We Hold
These Truths. . . .

WE HOLD THESE TRUTHS. . . .

AND OTHER WORDS THAT MADE AMERICA

PAUL ARON

WITH ILLUSTRATIONS BY DAVID SMITH

ROWMAN & LITTLEFIELD PUBLISHERS, INC.
Lanham • Boulder • New York • Toronto • Plymouth, UK

In association with
THE COLONIAL
WILLIAMSBURG FOUNDATION
Williamsburg, Virginia

Colonial Williamsburg

ROWMAN & LITTLEFIELD PUBLISHERS, INC.

In association with THE COLONIAL WILLIAMSBURG FOUNDATION
P.O. Box 1776
Williamsburg, VA 23187-1776
www. colonialwilliamsburg.org

Published in the United States of America
by Rowman & Littlefield Publishers, Inc.
A wholly owned subsidiary of The Rowman & Littlefield Publishing Group, Inc.
4501 Forbes Boulevard, Suite 200, Lanham, Maryland 20706
www.rowmanlittlefield.com

Estover Road
Plymouth PL6 7PY
United Kingdom

Distributed by National Book Network

973.3

A76W

2008

British Library Cataloguing in Publication Information Available

Library of Congress Cataloging-in-Publication Data

Aron, Paul, 1956–
    We hold these truths— : and other words that made America / Paul Aron.
        p. cm.
    Includes bibliographical references and index.
    ISBN-13: 978-0-7425-6272-1 (cloth : alk. paper)
    ISBN-10: 0-7425-6272-7 (cloth : alk. paper)
    eISBN-13: 978-0-7425-6559-3
    eISBN-10: 0-7425-6559-9
    1. United States—History—Revolution, 1775–1783—Miscellanea.
    2. United States—Quotations, maxims, etc. 3. Quotations, American.
    I. Title.
    E209.A76 2008
    973.3—dc22   2008021873

Printed in the United States of America

∞™ The paper used in this publication meets the minimum
requirements of American National Standard for Information
Sciences—Permanence of Paper for Printed Library Materials, ANSI/NISO
Z39.48-1992.

Contents

v

PREFACE

THOMAS JEFFERSON did not want to write the Declaration of Independence. He did not even want to be at the Continental Congress in Philadelphia. He would have much preferred to be in Williamsburg, where delegates to the Virginia Convention were drafting a constitution for the newly independent commonwealth. Yet John Adams, who wished he could write the Declaration himself, admitted that he had been so "obnoxious" in his zeal for independence that any draft he wrote "would undergo a more severe scrutiny and criticism in Congress." So, Adams insisted, it had to be Jefferson.

Within a day or two, Jefferson produced a draft. Just a few weeks later, Congress, especially Adams and Benjamin Franklin, completed the editing, and Jefferson's words took on their familiar form: "We hold these truths to be self evident, that all men are created equal, that they are endowed by their Creator with certain unalienable Rights, that among these are life, liberty and the pursuit of happiness."

How Jefferson reluctantly yet speedily composed the Declaration, how he drew upon the work of others such as George Mason and John Milton and John Locke, how Congress handled the editing (or, as Jefferson felt at the time, the "mutilations") of the Declaration: these are among the stories told in this book. They are worth telling, for, despite the fame of Jefferson's words, the stories behind them are surprising and revealing.

The same can be said for the words of our other founding fathers (and of the occasional founding mother). Few know, for example, that Patrick Henry may never have said "If this be treason, make the most of it" or that Paul Revere surely never said "the British are coming." Few know where Benjamin Franklin found his "Poor Richard" proverbs, such as "Early to bed, and early to rise, / Makes a man, healthy, wealthy and wise." Few know how the (entirely fictional) tale of George Washington admitting he cut down the cherry tree originated and spread or how James Otis's declaration that "taxation without representation is tyranny" led to his going insane. Few have even heard of James Wilson, whose "We the people" opens the Constitution.

The stories behind these words will, I hope, entertain you. But they are also worth reading because these words mattered. True, the American Revolution did not end slavery or poverty. True, too, America's birth meant death for many American Indians, and women remained second-class citizens until at least the twentieth century. Such truths have led many to think of the words of the founding fathers as hypocrisy. "How is it," asked Samuel Johnson in 1775, "that we hear the loudest yelps for liberty among the drivers of Negroes?" The self-evident truths of Thomas Jefferson's Declaration of Independence were, some have argued, no more than an elegant screen covering the colonists' struggle for power or, even more cynically, their desire to renege on their debts to British merchants.

Yet these words continued to reverberate long after the Revolution. However short they fell of their own ideals, those who spoke or wrote them truly believed they were struggling against tyranny. "Americans were involved," wrote historian Gordon Wood, "not simply in a defense of their own rights, but in a worldwide struggle for the salvation of liberty itself." The Revolution created not only a new nation but also a new way of thinking, one in which people were no longer subjects of a king but citizens of a republic. As Thomas Paine put it in 1782: "We see with other eyes; we hear with other ears; and think with other thoughts, than those we formerly used."

The words of Paine—and of Franklin and Henry and Washington and others in this book—have inspired people to work for a world where Jefferson's self-evident truths are universally recognized, where all men really are created equal. The words whose stories are told here are the words through which our founders defined and refined the nature of our government and society. These are the words that changed the course of history.

These are the words that made America.

*A*CKNOWLEDGMENTS

FOR THEIR advice and support, thanks to Christopher Anzalone, Stephen Aron, Laura Barry, Linda Baumgarten, John Corrigan, John Galvin, Ronald Hurst, Kevin Kelly, Richard McCluney, Wolfgang Mieder, Ashlee Mills, Piper Wallis, John Waters Jr., and Amy Watson.

I am especially grateful for the careful readings and thoughtful comments of Joseph Rountree and Linda Rowe.

CHAPTER I

ABIGAIL ADAMS

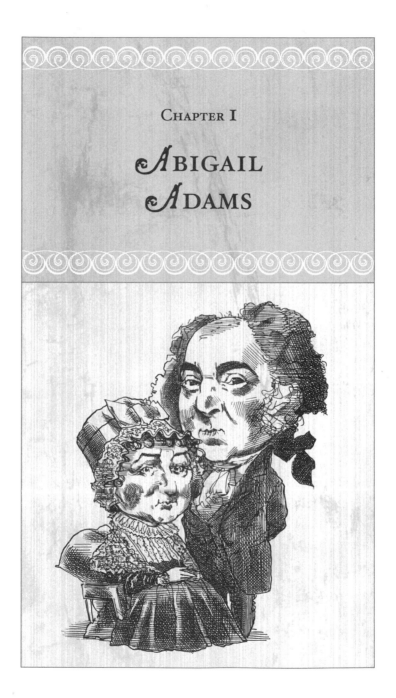

"Remember the Ladies"

I LONG TO hear that you have declared an independency," wrote Abigail Adams in a March 1776 letter to
her husband John, then a delegate to the Continental
Congress in Philadelphia. "And by the way," she continued,

> in the new Code of Laws which I suppose it will be
> necessary for you to make I desire you would Remem-
> ber the Ladies, and be more generous and favorable
> to them than your ancestors. Do not put such unlim-
> ited power into the hands of the husbands. Remem-
> ber all men would be tyrants if they could. If particular
> care and attention is not paid to the ladies we are
> determined to foment a rebellion, and will not hold
> ourselves bound by any laws in which we have no
> voice, or representation.

In her life as well as her letters, Abigail Adams pushed
the limits of what women of the era were expected to do.
With her husband away on political business for months at
a time, she not only raised four children largely on her own
but also managed the family farm and investments, including hiring, firing, and supervising workers. She did not hesitate to give her husband political advice, as evidenced in
hundreds of letters. "If a woman does not hold the reigns
of government," she wrote her sister Elizabeth Peabody in
1799 (while John Adams was president), "I see no reason for
her not judging how they are conducted."

John Adams's response was often to tease his wife. Answering her "Remember the Ladies" letter, he wrote that he'd heard the Revolution had "loosened the bands of government every where," including among Indians and Negroes. This, however, was "the first intimation that another tribe more numerous and powerful than all the rest were grown discontented." To her threat that women might someday rebel, he responded with mock fear: "We have only the name of Masters, and rather than give up this, which would completely subject us to the despotism of the petticoat, I hope General Washington, and all our brave heroes would fight."

This wasn't the response Abigail Adams hoped for, and she confided to her friend Mercy Otis Warren that he was "very sausy." To John, she responded with a tone that was lighthearted but insistent.

"I can not say that I think you are very generous to the ladies," she retorted, "for whilst you are proclaiming peace and good will to men, emancipating all nations, you insist upon retaining an absolute power over wives. But you must remember that arbitrary power is like most other things which are very hard, very liable to be broken."

Such words have led some historians and biographers to portray Adams as a twentieth-century suffragette or twenty-first-century feminist living in the eighteenth and nineteenth centuries. These she most definitely was not. Her March 1776 letter to her husband did not call for voting rights or for a woman's right to hold public office or even to attend town meetings. What she most likely had in mind, though she did not specify them, were the rights to choose a husband and to leave an abusive one, to share in the fruits of their mutual labor, and perhaps to educate oneself and one's daughters. At no point did she call for a fundamental change in men's and women's roles. When she wrote John about the farm, she referred to "his" business affairs. Even when she wrote of politics, clearly with passion and knowledge, she conceded it was a male domain. She believed that women could participate in politics by influencing their husbands and sons and that this was a perfectly equitable arrangement. "Let each planet shine in their own orbit, God and nature designed it so," she wrote her sister in 1799. "If man is Lord, woman is *Lordess*—that is what I contend for."

"However brilliant a woman's talents may be," she wrote to her son John Quincy in 1796, "she ought never to shine at the expence of her husband. Government of states and kingdoms, tho God knows badly enough managed, I am willing should be solely administered by Lords of the Creation."

If anything, she became more conservative as she aged. "No man ever prospered in the world without the consent and cooperation of his wife," she wrote her sister Elizabeth in 1809. "I consider it as an indispensable requisite, that every American wife should herself know how to order and regulate her family; how to govern her domestics, and train up her children. For this purpose, the all-wise Creator made woman an helpmeet for man, and she who fails in these duties does not answer the end of her creation."

Abigail Adams lived by these precepts. Throughout her life, she rose at five in the morning, did her own sewing, and churned her own butter. As First Lady, she worried she would not live up to the conventionally feminine example of Martha Washington. Though she was undeniably sincere in asking the Continental Congress to "Remember the Ladies," she did not take the threat of a ladies' "rebellion" any more seriously than her husband.

It was not as if she was unfamiliar with more radical ideas of equality. Abigail and John Adams both read Mary

Wollstonecraft's 1792 *Vindication of the Rights of Women*. Wollstonecraft, a British political theorist, argued that women deserved equal opportunities in work and politics. Indeed, in 1794, after Abigail once again badgered John about women's rights, he teasingly called her a "disciple" of Wollstonecraft.

A Virginian, Hannah Lee Corbin, also took a more radical stance than Abigail's. Like Abigail, Corbin was related to a key Revolutionary figure; her brother Richard Henry Lee introduced the resolution for independence in the Continental Congress. Corbin tested her brother's tolerance at least as much as Abigail did her husband's. As a widow, Corbin lived openly with a widower named Richard Hall. They may have been married in a Baptist ceremony, which to the Anglican Lees would have been almost as bad as not being married at all. Of Corbin's support for women's suffrage, we have only indirect but nonetheless substantive evidence—a 1778 letter from Richard Henry Lee telling his sister that he agreed with her letter (a letter which has never been found) and that widows and unmarried women with property should be able to vote. Richard Henry did note a practical problem: namely, that votes were cast aloud and in public, and that it would be "rather out of character for women to press into those tumultuous assemblages of men where the business of choosing representatives is conducted."

Richard Henry Lee was, for his time, open-minded on the subject of women's rights. So was John Adams; despite his teasing, he genuinely respected—indeed depended on—his wife's opinions. "I never wanted your advice and assistance more in my life," he wrote after his presidential inauguration. And soon after that: "The times are critical and dangerous, and I must have you here to assist me."

Abigail recognized that she was fortunate in her choice of a husband. Her own family presented clear examples of bad marriages. Her sister married an alcoholic; her daughter married an irresponsible spendthrift; her son, John Quincy Adams, though highly accomplished (he followed in his father's footsteps and became president), was a cold and domineering husband. Abigail and John, in contrast, shared respect and love. "O that I could annihilate space," she wrote in May 1776, bemoaning that they were still apart. And he to her two months later: "I feel every generous passion and every kind of sentiment, rushing for utterance, while I subscribe myself yours."

Despite his condescending response to her "Remember the Ladies" letter, Abigail did succeed in chipping away at his male chauvinism. That much is clear from his May 1776 letter to James Sullivan. Sullivan had proposed allowing men without property to vote. Adams argued, quite logically, that, if you gave men without property the vote, you'd have to give it to women as well, since "generally speaking, women . . . have as good judgments, and as independent minds, as those men who are wholly destitute of property."

This was hardly an endorsement of women's suffrage, a position neither Adams ever advocated. It was not until more than a century later, in 1920, that states ratified the Nineteenth Amendment to the Constitution, finally giving women the right to vote. But our founding fathers and mothers were already thinking about the issue, and that was in part due to Abigail Adams.

CHAPTER 2

JOHN ADAMS

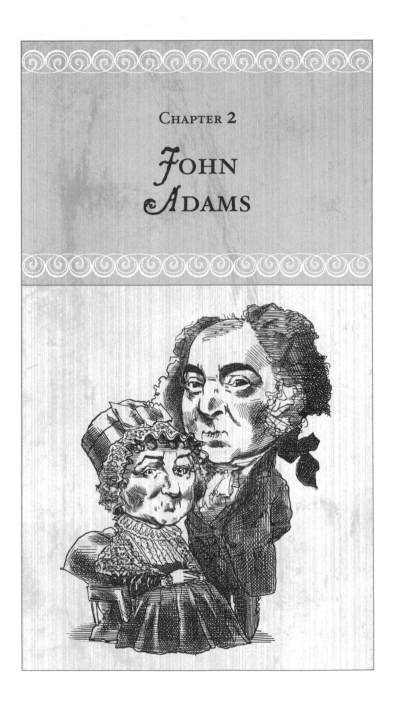

"Facts are stubborn things"

ON MARCH 5, 1770, British soldiers under the command of Captain Thomas Preston fired into a crowd, killing three Bostonians and mortally wounding two others. The "Boston Massacre" quickly became a rallying point for Americans. Paul Revere produced an engraving showing soldiers firing point-blank at civilians, and that was used as the frontispiece for "A Short Narrative of the Horrid Massacre in Boston," a pamphlet published by the town. To make sure the image didn't fade from American memory, Samuel Adams set aside March 5th as a day of mourning.

Yet, when the British soldiers were tried for murder, their defense attorney was none other than Sam Adams's cousin John Adams. He described the massacre's victims as "a motley rabble of saucy boys, Negroes and mulattoes, Irish teagues and outlandish jacktars." They were not even a mob, Adams maintained, since "the name is too respectable for them."

On December 3rd, in his closing argument to the jury, Adams continued to blame the victims, describing how the rabble had pelted the soldiers with snowballs, oyster shells, and sticks, threatened to kill them, and hit one soldier with a club. The deaths, Adams maintained, were a clear case of self-defense.

"Facts are stubborn things," he concluded, "and whatever may be our wishes, our inclinations, or the dictums of our passions, they cannot alter the state of facts and evidence."

How was it that the future Revolutionary leader came to defend the British?

Adams himself recalled, thirty years later, that he was sitting in his office when he was visited by a merchant sympathetic to the British soldiers. "With tears streaming from his eyes, he said I am come with a very solemn message from a very unfortunate man, Captain Preston in prison," Adams wrote. "He wishes for counsel, and can get none."

"I had no hesitation in answering that counsel ought to be the very last thing that an accused person should [lack] in a free country," Adams told the merchant.

Adams's reputation as one of Boston's best lawyers was well deserved. During Preston's trial, prosecution witnesses testified they heard the captain give the order to fire. Adams's cross-examination raised the possibility that what Preston had said was "fire by no means," even if some in the crowd heard only the first word. Adams also paraded to the stand a series of defense witnesses. Especially effective was Richard Palmes, a merchant who had attacked Preston and was standing right next to him when the shooting began, yet conceded he had never heard the captain order the soldiers to fire.

The jury took only three hours to acquit Preston.

Next came the trial of the rest of the soldiers. Adams faced a tricky problem. Having established that Preston never gave the order to fire, he had eliminated the soldiers' best defense; namely, that they were just following orders.

Adams and his co-counsel, Josiah Quincy, called a series of witnesses to testify about the dangerous situation in which the soldiers found themselves. The strategy worked—this time the jury took only two and a half hours to acquit six of the soldiers of murder. Two others were found guilty of the lesser charge of manslaughter. They were sentenced to having their thumbs branded, a painful punishment but one that avoided any jail time.

Outside the courtroom the "stubborn facts" of the case remained in dispute. Samuel Adams, writing in the *Boston Gazette*, decried a miscarriage of justice and demanded revenge. Many blamed John Adams. In 1822 he recalled, somewhat bitterly, that he and Quincy "heard our names execrated in the most opprobrious terms whenever we appeared in the streets of Boston." Half his clients, Adams said, deserted his practice. "To this hour," he wrote in 1815, "my conduct . . . is alleged against me to prove I am an enemy to my country, and always have been." Even Preston showed no gratitude. The British captain was understand-ably eager to get out of Boston and saw Adams only once again, years later, when they passed each other on a Lon-don street. Adams's total compensation for both cases, he later grumbled, was eighteen guineas.

Still, for many colonists, the trials were as much a prop-aganda victory as a legal defeat. If the massacre proved the evils of British power, the verdicts proved the power of American justice. They should, Samuel Adams's friend Samuel Cooper wrote Benjamin Franklin, "wipe off the imputation of our being so violent and bloodthirsty a peo-ple, as not to permit law and justice to take place on the side of unpopular men." And despite Adams's characteristic crankiness, in the long run he had no reason to regret his commitment to the principle that no accused person should lack counsel. The trial solidified his reputation for integrity. He wrote in his autobiography that, "although the clamor was very loud among some sorts of people, it has been a great consolation to me, through life, that I acted in this business with steady impartiality, and conducted it to so happy an issue."

"the most insignificant office that ever the invention of man contrived"

Less happy for Adams was his tenure as vice president. To his wife, Abigail, he described the vice presidency as "the most insignificant office that ever the invention of man contrived or his imagination conceived." In his diary, Senator William Maclay of Pennsylvania recorded Adams's complaints: "I feel a great difficulty how to act. I am Vice President, in this I am nothing, but I may be everything."

Congress apparently agreed: it allocated only $5,000 for the vice president's salary, one-fifth what the president would be paid. One senator argued that even that amount was too much, since the vice president could discharge most of his duties from his own home. For Adams, who liked to be in the thick of things, part of the problem was that the vice president had no clear role other than to break the rare tie in the Senate, or to wait around in case the president died.

Adams could not resist joining in one of the Senate's first debates, and he quickly came to regret it. The issue was what to call the president and vice president. Adams, defending not only his own sense of dignity but also that of George Washington, insisted on titles that would properly honor statesmen and impress foreign governments. Adams had in mind something like "His Majesty." A committee of senators came up with "His Highness the President of the United States of America and Protector of their Liberties." To the majority of Americans, who after all had only recently gotten rid of a king, this smacked of monarchism. Thomas Jefferson called the committee's title "the most superlatively ridiculous thing I ever heard of." Maclay called Adams "silly" and "vain," saying his "pride, obstinacy and folly are equal to his vanity." Others were more irreverent: some senators started jokingly referring to each other as "Highness of the Senate" and to Adams as "His Rotundity."

Ultimately, the Senate and House settled on simply "The President of the United States." For Adams's opponents, though, his insistence on titles revealed a disturbing sympathy for monarchy. Indeed, Adams had a very different view of democracy than many Americans. As early as 1770, when he defended the British soldiers accused in the Boston Massacre, Adams exhibited his faith in the rule of law and his fear of an unchecked mob. Democrats like Jefferson and Thomas Paine could embrace the "will of the people" as an unquestioned good. Not Adams, especially after the French Revolution confirmed his worst fears.

"That all men are born to equal rights is true," Adams conceded in his 1787 *Defence of the Constitutions of Government of the United States of America*. "But to teach that all men are born with equal powers and faculties, to equal influence in society . . . is as gross a fraud . . . as ever was practiced by . . . the self-styled philosophers of the French Revolution." Adams described fifty babies in a single room, all four days old, all in identical cradles, all dressed and nursed alike, yet all strikingly different. "They were born to equal rights," he concluded, "but to very different fortunes; to very different success and influence in life."

Democrats like Jefferson and Paine couldn't just wish away class differences, Adams argued. Just because America had no feudal heritage didn't mean there was no elite. This "natural aristocracy" had its place in a republic—specifically, the Senate. The majority had its voice in the House of Representatives. And both the majority and the minority needed to be kept in check by a powerful presidency.

Adams did not deny that a government's power ought to come from "the people." Where he broke with more radical democrats was in insisting that the people—and the aristocracy—were potentially as great a danger as a king. "The fundamental article of my political creed," he wrote Jefferson in 1816, "is, that despotism, or unlimited sovereignty, or absolute power is the same in a majority of a popular assembly, an aristocratical counsel, an oligarchical junto and a single emperor."

Adams was advocating a system of checks and balances that remains a key part of American democracy. He saw himself as defending the Constitution; indeed, as defending the rule of law against attacks from left and right. He was, however, noticeably out of step with the majority of Americans, who thought class distinctions had no place in America and who saw kings and aristocrats, not ordinary people, as the greatest danger to their freedom. In her 1805 *History of the American Revolution*, Mercy Otis Warren, amidst what was overall a positive assessment of Adams's contribution to the Revolution, wrote that during his various diplomatic missions to Europe, "by living long near the splendor of courts and courtiers" he became "beclouded by a partiality for monarchy." This resulted in "a lapse from [his] former republican principles."

Adams furiously denied the charge. In an 1807 letter to Warren, Adams challenged "the whole human race, and angels and devils too, to produce an instance of [his monarchical sympathies] from my cradle to this hour." In another letter to Warren (he wrote ten in response to her book), he reiterated the key roles he had played in creating the American republic: it was he who wrote the decisive motion in the Continental Congress, it was he who negotiated the treaty that ended the war, it was he whose writings provided the model for the Constitution, it was he who had "done more labor, run through more and greater dangers, and made greater sacrifices than any man among my contemporaries living or dead, in the service of my country."

Adams's claims were certainly exaggerated, ignoring the facts that Richard Henry Lee introduced the motion for independence and that Benjamin Franklin played a key role in negotiating the treaty. These were not the words of an objective historian. These were the words of a man deeply wounded by his country's failure to understand and appreciate him.

"The Revolution was in the minds and hearts of the people"

Adams was always jealous of his fellow founding fathers. He complained to Benjamin Rush in 1790 that the only things people would know about the Revolution "will be that Dr. Franklin's electrical rod smote the earth and out sprung George Washington." He was especially worried that, instead of his painstaking efforts to secure the Continental Congress's support for independence, it would be Jefferson's Declaration that would be remembered. "Was there ever a coup de theatre, that had so great an effect as Jefferson's penmanship of the Declaration of Independence?" he wrote Rush. To William Cunningham, he referred to the Declaration as "a theatrical side show," complaining that "Jefferson ran away with the stage effect . . . and all the glory of it."

In Adams's view, history was putting Virginians like Jefferson and Patrick Henry at center stage at the expense of New Englanders like James Otis, John Hancock, Samuel Adams, and of course himself. William Wirt's celebratory biography of Henry, written in 1817, so irked Adams that a year later he sent a letter to Hezekiah Niles's *Weekly Register*. The letter contained Adams's most famous words on the Revolution.

"But what do we mean by the American Revolution?" Adams wrote. "Do we mean the American war? The Revolution was effected before the war commenced. The Revolution was in the minds and hearts of the people."

To some extent, Adams was again stressing the key role he and his fellow New Englanders played in mobilizing the colonies to create a united front against Great Britain. "Thirteen clocks were made to strike together," he wrote Niles in the same letter.

Yet Adams's words ought not to be reduced to mere self-promotion. They were also an important analysis of how the Revolution came about. The Revolution was the result of more than Adams's lobbying or Jefferson's writing. It was the result of a change in attitude, one that took place over years. Gradually, between 1760 and 1775, in Adams's opinion, Americans came to think of themselves not as subjects of the king but as citizens of a free nation. The Declaration reflected this change, but it did not cause it.

"This radical change in the principles, opinions, sentiments, and affections of the people was the real American Revolution," Adams wrote Niles.

"Thomas Jefferson survives"

Adams and Jefferson, close allies during the Revolution, became bitter enemies after. They represented opposing views of democracy, "the North and South Poles of the American Revolution," as Rush put it. Adams, always fearful of "the people," would never accept Jefferson's dictum that "governments are republican only in proportion as they embody the will of the people, and execute it." Adams was not, despite what his opponents said, a monarchist; indeed, he led a revolution against a king as well as a parliament. He did, however, believe that a strong executive was essential to constrain "the people," who presented at least as great a danger to democracy as any king. The French Revolution, he was sure, proved his case.

It did not help their relationship that Jefferson defeated Adams in the 1800 presidential election.

Gradually, however, they put aside their differences, and eventually the two reconciled. "You and I ought not to die, before we have explained ourselves to each other," Adams wrote Jefferson in 1813. For the rest of their lives, through 158 letters, they attempted to do so. The letters are often lighthearted—Adams liked to refer to his comparatively humble home as "Montezillo," in contrast to Jefferson's Monticello—and equally often profound. They were, historian Joseph Ellis wrote, "a landmark in American letters and eventually a classic . . . statement of the founding generation."

In a coincidence almost too amazing to be believed, both Adams and Jefferson died on July 4, 1826, the fiftieth anniversary of independence. A few days before, a delegation of local leaders called on Adams to ask how they might toast the Fourth. "I will give you," Adams offered, "Independence forever!"

Adams's last words, spoken at about 5:30 in the afternoon and moments before he died, were: "Thomas Jefferson survives." Actually, Jefferson had died a little after noon.

CHAPTER 3

ANONYMOUS

"E Pluribus Unum"

HAVING DECLARED independence, the Continental Congress needed an emblem for the new nation. On July 4, 1776, Congress named John Adams, Benjamin Franklin, and Thomas Jefferson—three of the five men who had been assigned to draft the Declaration of Independence—to a committee charged with designing "a device for a seal for the United States of America." This turned out to be a much more time-consuming task than the Declaration.

From a letter from Adams to his wife, Abigail, we know that Adams suggested a picture of Hercules and Jefferson a picture of the children of Israel in the wilderness. Franklin wanted a picture of Moses parting the Red Sea and Pharaoh being engulfed by its waters, along with the motto "Rebellion to tyrants is obedience to God." Unable to agree, the committee consulted with a Swiss-born artist named Pierre Eugene Du Simitiere. On August 20th, the committee presented its recommendation to Congress. The design included the Latin words *E Pluribus Unum*—out of many, one. Congress didn't think much of the proposal and simply ignored it. Congress was equally dissatisfied with the proposal of a second committee in 1780 and a third in 1782.

Frustrated, Congress turned the problem over to its secretary, Charles Thomson. Thomson incorporated features of all previous designs, giving the bald eagle its prominent place on the seal and bringing back *E Pluribus Unum* from the first design. He added two other Latin phrases to the seal: *Annuit Coeptis* (He has favored our undertakings) and *Novus Ordo Seclorum* (A new order of the ages). Finally, six years after appointing the first committee, Congress approved Thomson's version of the seal.

The significance of *E Pluribus Unum* was clear: out of many (i.e., thirteen states) came one (i.e., one nation). The origins of the phrase, however, are much murkier. Some scholars traced it back to the Roman poet Virgil, whose *Moretum* tells of a farmer who mixes various ingredients into a salad dressing. The poem includes the phrase *color est e pluribus unus*. But the words are not exactly the same and the context is very different: Virgil was describing how out of many (in this case, many herbs and other ingredients) would come one (in this case, a dressing of a single color). This seemed an unlikely inspiration for a motto on a great seal. As classicist Monroe E. Deutsch put it, "The thought of a 'salad of states' hardly seems a happy or appropriate one, or likely to seem so to men who had completed the Declaration of Independence but a month and a half before." Other theories traced the phrase to Horace, another Roman poet, or Augustine, the Christian philosopher, but, like Virgil's, their words were similar but not identical to those of the great seal, and the contexts were very different. Besides, though many of the founders were well versed in the classics, there is no evidence that any member of the committee was thinking of any of these versions.

What they probably were thinking of was the *Gentleman's Magazine*, published in London and read on both sides of the Atlantic. The title page of that magazine displayed the exact phrase: *E Pluribus Unum*. The 1734 edition of the magazine explained its choice of the phrase in verse: "To your motto most true, for our monthly inspection, / You mix various rich sweets in one fragrant collection." The magazine may have been inspired by Virgil or Augustine or Horace, but the committee more likely took the words from the magazine than from some classical source.

Who first suggested the motto is also murky. Some have credited Du Simitiere on the grounds that he drew the sketch that included the motto, but Du Simitiere was a painter and a foreigner. Adams and Franklin and Jefferson, on the other hand, were members of the committee assigned the job. Deutsch gave the nod to Franklin, partly because Franklin's articles had frequently appeared in the *Gentleman's Magazine*. Besides, Franklin clearly had a knack for mottoes: witness, for example, his suggestion of "Rebellion to tyrants is obedience to God" or his earlier coining of "Join or Die."

Whatever its origins, the meaning of *E Pluribus Unum* has changed over time. Instead of just the unity of states, it also has come to signify and celebrate the unity of an increasingly diverse American people. As such, it would be perfectly appropriate had the words reached America's great seal via a British magazine and a Swiss-born artist.

"Yankee Doodle went to town"

Like the lyrics themselves, most theories about the origins of the words to "Yankee Doodle" don't make a lot of sense. The etymology of *yankee* is particularly murky.

Some traced the word to various Indian roots. One theory suggested there was a tribe known as the Yankoos, whom the colonists found very difficult to defeat, but there's no evidence of a tribe by that name. Another concluded it came from the Cherokee word *eankke*, though such a word does not exist. The most widely accepted of the Indian etymologies, according to the *Oxford English Dictionary*, is that it was a corruption of the word *English*, though it seems quite a stretch from *English* to *Yankee*.

Yankee has also been traced to the Persian *janghe*—as in Jenghis or Genghis Khan. More credibly, some favored a

Dutch etymology, arguing that the Dutch colonists in New
York called New Englanders *Jankes* (perhaps a diminutive
form of *Jan* or *Johnnie*) and that the lyrics to the song originated not from hostility between English and Americans
but between English and Dutch.

Doodle is easier to explain—a doodle was a silly person
or country bumpkin, sort of a noodle. Which ought not to
be mistaken for *macaroni*, which in the song referred not to
pasta but to someone who dressed in an affected manner,
sort of a dandy. An 1824 account of the song's history credited Dr.
Richard Shuckburgh, a British military surgeon, with com-
posing the lyrics or the tune in 1755, though versions of both
existed before then. Like many folk songs, this one clearly
evolved over decades until someone, perhaps Shuckburgh,
decided that Yankee Doodle came to town riding on his
pony and then, inexplicably, stuck a feather in his hat and
called it macaroni.

Whatever the song's origins, during the Revolution it was
British troops who first marched to "Yankee Doodle," presumably to ridicule the country bumpkins who thought they
could take on the much better trained, not to mention better
dressed, forces. While pushing back the British from Lexington and Concord, the rebels appropriated the tune, and it
soon became an unofficial American anthem. The *Massachusetts Spy* of May 20, 1775, offered the following report:

> When the second brigade marched out of Boston to
> reinforce the first, nothing was played by the fifes and
> drums but *Yankee Doodle*. . . . Upon their return to
> Boston, one asked his brother officer how he liked
> the tune now,—"D–n them! returned he, *they made us
> dance it till we were tired.*"—Since which *Yankee Doo-
> dle* sounds less sweet to their ears.

CHAPTER 4

JOHN DICKINSON

"By uniting we stand, by dividing we fall"

IN DECEMBER 1767 a letter appeared in the *Pennsylvania Chronicle* signed merely "A Farmer." Eleven more letters quickly followed, all warning of the danger to Americans posed by recent acts of Parliament. In particular, the letters assailed Britain's taxation of the colonies, its standing army, and its government's corruption.

"Whoever seriously considers the matter," the farmer wrote in his first letter, "must perceive that a dreadful stroke is aimed at the liberty of these colonies. I say, of these colonies; for the cause of *one* is the cause of *all*."

The farmer's words soon spread through all the colonies. Nineteen of the twenty-three colonial newspapers printed all of them, and in 1768 they were compiled as "Letters from a Pennsylvania Farmer" and published in pamphlet form in New York, Boston, Williamsburg (with a preface by Richard Henry Lee, who eight years later would introduce the resolution for independence at the Continental Congress), London, and Paris (the last two with a preface by Benjamin Franklin). The farmer was toasted throughout America. At a town meeting, Boston voted "that the thanks of the town be given to the ingenious author of a course of letters . . . wherein the rights of the American subjects are clearly stated and fully vindicated" and appointed John Hancock and Samuel Adams to a committee assigned to publish a letter stating Boston's gratitude.

The letter writer, it was soon revealed, was John Dickinson, a Philadelphia lawyer and legislator who owned a farm on the banks of the Delaware River. The letters made Dickinson a leading proponent of American rights. Patience Wright made a wax model of him and Paul Revere an engraving. No other Revolutionary pamphlet, except Thomas Paine's "Common Sense" in 1776, had an impact comparable to that of the "Letters."

Soon after finishing the last of the letters, Dickinson turned to songwriting. In July 1768, he sent James Otis of Boston a poem to be sung to an old English tune called "Hearts of Oak." The chorus went:

In freedom we're born, and in freedom we'll live,
Our purses are ready,
Steady, friends, steady.
Not as slaves, but as freemen our money we'll give.

In the sixth stanza, Dickinson again called for unity among the colonists:

Then join hand in hand brave Americans all,
By *uniting* we stand, by *dividing* we fall;
In so righteous a cause let us hope to succeed,
For heaven approves of each generous deed—

The song, like the letters, struck a chord. Otis forwarded it to the *Boston Gazette*, which printed it. Under various titles, including "The Freedom Song," "The Liberty Song," and "The New Song for American Freedom," it was reprinted and sung across the colonies. In Massachusetts, John Adams praised the song for "cultivating the sensations of freedom." In Virginia, Richard Henry Lee's brother Arthur circulated it throughout the colony. (Arthur Lee had been so impressed with the "Letters" that he had introduced himself to Dickinson and then contributed eight of the lines to the song.)

"United, we stand—Divided, we fall"

In 1776, Dickinson's words were still resonating throughout America. In Williamsburg, two days after the Virginia Convention passed a resolution instructing its delegates to introduce a declaration of independence at the Continental Congress in Philadelphia, editor Alexander Purdie replaced the coat of arms that had served as its masthead for the *Virginia Gazette*. Instead, Purdie inserted these words:

> Thirteen United Colonies.
> United, we stand—Divided, we fall.

Dickinson himself would not in the end stand with the Adamses and the Lees and other patriot leaders. Though he continued to protest British policies, he was at heart a conservative eager to preserve the colonists' traditional rights as British subjects, not to establish new rights as American citizens. The farmer's letters had suggested "constitutional modes of obtaining relief," not outright rebellion. Dickinson was unwilling to risk war with England, at least without first securing an alliance with the French. On July 1, 1776, he stood before the Continental Congress and warned his fellow delegates that to declare independence prematurely would be to "brave the storm in a skiff of paper." He urged "deliberation, wisdom, caution, and unanimity."

Dickinson realized the tide of independence could not be turned back. He could not bring himself to vote for independence, but he still understood the value of unity.

When the resolution came to a vote on July 2nd, Dickinson and his fellow Pennsylvania conservative, Robert Morris, abstained. This allowed the colony's delegates to vote 3 to 2 in favor of independence and allowed Congress to report that the Declaration of Independence had passed "without a single dissenting" vote from any of the colonies.

As he addressed Congress on July 1st, Dickinson conceded his position would be "the finishing blow to my once too great and . . . now too diminished popularity." His prediction was correct: though he later served in the Philadelphia militia and signed the Constitution, his reputation never recovered. Thomas Jefferson called Dickinson "a lawyer of more ingenuity than sound judgment, and still more timid than ingenious." That is how he is still remembered.

CHAPTER 5

OLAUDAH EQUIANO

"The shrieks of the women, and the groans of the dying"

IN THE EIGHTEENTH century, England dominated the seas and the transatlantic slave trade. Nearly six million Africans were brought to the Americas in chains during those hundred years, about half of them in British ships. Yet, by the late 1780s, the abolitionist movement in England (which at that point focused on ending the slave trade as opposed to freeing all slaves) was building momentum. The evangelical Christian William Wilberforce led the fight in the House of Commons. Outside Parliament, the radical Thomas Clarkson and the scholarly Granville Sharp organized Quakers and others. Pottery designer and manufacturer Josiah Wedgwood created an image, which served as the movement's informal logo, of a kneeling African in chains encircled by the words "Am I Not a Man and a Brother?" Perhaps more than any of these, the man whose words pushed England to end the slave trade was a former slave, Olaudah Equiano. Equiano's autobiography, *The Interesting Narrative of the Life of Olaudah Equiano or Gustavus Vassa, the African*, was published in 1789.

Equiano was not the first African to write about slavery; two years earlier, Equiano's friend Quobna Ottobah Cugoano had published *Thoughts and Sentiments on the Evil and Wicked Traffic of the Slavery and Commerce of the Human Species*. Cugoano argued that slavery was immoral, as did Equiano in dozens of letters to newspapers, abolitionists, and Queen Charlotte (this last probably because he recognized King George III was intractably opposed to abolition). Equiano's autobiography, however, took a fundamentally different approach. Unlike Cugoano's book or Equiano's letters, *The Interesting Narrative* did not analyze the morality of slavery but instead described its horrors. Of all Equiano's words, the most quoted were those about the Middle Passage, the journey to America:

> The stench of the hold while we were on the coast was so intolerably loathsome, that it was dangerous to remain there for any time, and some of us had been permitted to stay on the deck for the fresh air; but now that the whole ship's cargo were confined together, it became absolutely pestilential. The closeness of the place, and the heat of the climate, added to the number in the ship, which was so crowded that each had scarcely room to turn himself, almost suffocated us. This produced copious perspirations, so that the air soon became unfit for respiration, from a variety of loathsome smells, and brought on a sickness among the slaves, of which many died, thus falling victims to the improvident avarice, as I may call it, of their purchasers. This wretched situation was again aggravated by the galling of the chains, now become insupportable; and the filth of the necessary tubs [latrines], into which the children often fell, and were almost suffocated. The shrieks of the women, and the groans of the dying, rendered the whole scene of horror almost inconceivable.

This was not the first time British citizens, especially abolitionists, had heard about the Middle Passage. But it was the first time they had heard a firsthand account from a slave who experienced the journey. *The Interesting Narrative* became a bestseller. With Equiano as its African voice, the abolitionist movement enlisted the support of hundreds of thousands of British citizens who boycotted slave-grown sugar and signed petitions.

Equiano's story opened in Africa, in what is now southeastern Nigeria. The setting was pastoral, almost idyllic: "a charming fruitful vale, named Essaka," where Equiano was the son of the chief. When he was eleven years old, Equiano was kidnapped and sold, through various intermediaries, to the owner of a slave ship. On board, the misery was unbearable. Slaves threw themselves overboard in an attempt to commit suicide; those who were pulled out of the water were then flogged. When Equiano tried to starve himself, he was beaten.

Most of the slaves were sold in the West Indies, but the buyers there rejected Equiano as too young and too weak. He was shipped to Virginia, up the York River, "where we saw few or none of our native Africans, and not one soul who could talk to me." He was sold to a Virginia planter, then to a British naval officer who renamed him Gustavus Vassa. (Vassa was a medieval king of Sweden; like many slave names, this was intended to be ironic.) For six years, Equiano was a servant on various naval warships.

In the West Indies, Equiano was sold again, this time to a merchant. He witnessed many acts of cruelty but seized the chance to make some small side deals while traveling on his master's behalf. He saved enough so that in 1766, on the Caribbean island of Montserrat, he was able to buy his own freedom. "I who had been a slave in the morning, trembling at the will of another," he wrote, "now became my own master, and completely free. I thought this was the happiest day I had ever experienced." He set back to sea, enlisting on ships bound for, among other places, North America, the Mediterranean, and the Arctic. (He came within six hundred miles of the North Pole.) He eventually settled in England where he married an English-woman, accumulated considerable wealth, and wrote his autobiography.

Recently, scholars have questioned whether Equiano's story, particularly his descriptions of Africa and the Middle Passage, was genuinely autobiographical. Vincent Carretta, a professor of English at the University of Maryland and the editor of the Penguin edition of Equiano's writings, concluded that Equiano was probably born not in Africa but in South Carolina. Carretta searched the records of St. Margaret's Church in Westminster, where Equiano was baptized in 1759, and discovered that he was listed as "Gustavus Vassa a Black born in Carolina 12 years old." Carretta also tracked down the muster book of the *Racehorse*, the ship on which Equiano sailed to the Arctic in 1773. It listed the seaman "Gustavus Weston" as being born in South Carolina. Carretta concluded that the early parts of *The Interesting Narrative* were a creative mix of oral history and research, "as much the biography of a people as . . . the autobiography of an individual."

It remains possible that *The Interesting Narrative* is entirely true and that in 1759 and 1773 Equiano, perhaps not yet willing to reveal the story of his African life, invented a South Carolina birth to tell those at St. Margaret's and aboard the *Racehorse*. Adam Hochschild, author of an acclaimed history of the British abolition movement, noted that those parts of *The Interesting Narrative* that could be independently corroborated—his accounts, for example, of various military engagements in which he participated during his voyages—turned out to be consistently accurate and that it would be highly unusual for an autobiographer who was otherwise so scrupulous to make up part of his story. Still, Carretta's shocking findings could not be easily dismissed. For Hochschild and for most Equiano scholars, it was impossible to know for sure.

If *The Interesting Narrative* is part fiction, it is a work of fiction that, by articulating the desire of Africans and African Americans to live as free people, profoundly influenced the course of history. On August 1, 1838, all slaves throughout the British Empire became free. In America, where the slave population was increasing on its own, the end of the slave trade did not create any immediate crisis for Southern planters. Still, British abolitionists were an inspiration for their American counterparts. And, while there's no evidence that the authors of later slave narratives, such as Frederick Douglass, read Equiano's, there's plenty of evidence that Douglass and other prominent American abolitionists modeled their movement on that of Clarkson and Sharpe and Equiano. In 1857, for example, Douglass declared August 1st "illustrious among all the days of the year."

"The fact that the unrivaled superpower of the era had freed its slaves made clear that slavery's days were numbered," wrote Hochschild. "Nowhere was that felt more than in the United States."

CHAPTER 6

BENJAMIN FRANKLIN

"Early to bed and early to rise"

GENERATIONS OF parents inspired their children—or perhaps annoyed them—by reciting Benjamin Franklin's maxim: "Early to bed and early to rise, makes a man healthy wealthy and wise."

Any parent who doubted Franklin was the source of this wisdom could confirm the attribution in the fifteenth edition of *Bartlett's Familiar Quotations*, edited by Emily Morison Beck and published in 1980. More recently, they could check E. D. Hirsch's *Dictionary of Cultural Literacy*, which describes this as "a saying of Benjamin Franklin in *Poor Richard's Almanack*."

Samuel Clemens's parents quoted Franklin to him so often that he took it upon himself to prove Franklin wrong:

> I know it is not so; because I have got up early in the station-house many and many a time, and got poorer and poorer for the next half a day, in consequence, instead of richer and richer. And sometimes. . . . I have seen the sun rise four times a week up there at Virginia, and so far from my growing healthier on account of it, I got to looking blue, and pulpy, and swelled, like a drowned man, and my relations grew alarmed and thought they were going to lose me. . . . And as far as becoming wiser is concerned, you might put all the wisdom I acquired in these experiments in your eye, without obstructing your vision any to speak of.

"You observe that I have put a stronger test on the matter than even Benjamin Franklin contemplated," Clemens (writing as Mark Twain) concluded in his 1864 essay, "and yet it would not work."

Beck and Hirsch and Twain were all wrong to credit (or blame) Franklin, who did not invent the "early to bed" proverb. True, he printed it in the 1735 edition of *Poor Richard's Almanack*, a compilation of weather predictions, events of the previous year, phases of the moon, and times of tides, sunrises, and sunsets—with maxims like this one mixed in—that Franklin published annually between 1733 and 1758. True too, he reprinted the same maxim, along with one hundred or so others culled from the previous editions, in the 1758 *Almanack*. At no point, however, did Franklin claim the proverb as his own, or even as that of his fictional alter ego, Poor Richard. In fact, in the 1758 edition Franklin explicitly wrote that, though "my vanity was wonderfully delighted" by people quoting Poor Richard's proverbs, "not a tenth part of the wisdom was my own . . . but rather the gleanings that I made of the sense of all ages and nations." And in 1788 Franklin repeated in his autobiography that Poor Richard's proverbs "contained the wisdom of many ages and nations."

Beck, the *Bartlett's* editor, should certainly have known better. Earlier editions of *Bartlett's* cited *Paroemiologia Anglo-Latina . . . or Proverbs English, and Latine*, a 1639 collection by John Clarke, as the source of the proverb. Franklin may have first seen it there or in James Howell's 1659 collection, *Paroimiografia*. He might also have come across slightly different wordings of the proverb in Robert Codrington's 1664 *Collection of Many Select, and Excellent Proverbs out of Several Languages* ("Early to Bed, and early to Rise, makes a Man healthful, wealthy, and wise") or in John Ray's 1670 *Compleat Collection of English Proverbs* ("Early to go to bed and

early to rise, makes a man healthy, wealthy, and wise").
Though we don't know for sure how widely available these
were or whether Franklin had copies of any of these, the
circumstantial evidence is overwhelming, especially for
Howell's *Paroimiografia*: as proverb historian Robert New-
comb demonstrated, about 150 of the proverbs that ended
up in *Poor Richard's Almanack* between 1733 and 1742 were
also in Howell's work.

What Franklin often did was take an old proverb and
make it pithier. He started with, for example, "Fresh fish
and new-come guests smell, but that they are three days
old" and turned it into "Fish and visitors stink in three
days." And "Three may keep a secret if two of them are
away" became, in Franklin's hands, "Three may keep a
secret if two of them are dead."

Franklin's flair for choosing and editing proverbs made
Poor Richard's a great success, and a remarkable number of
these continue to circulate today. They have lasted partly
because they're so entertaining and partly because so many
of them appealed to an emerging middle class that valued
common sense and hard work. Just a sampling makes the
point: "Necessity never made a good bargain." "The sleep-
ing fox catches no poultry." "Diligence is the mother of
good luck." "Haste makes waste." "No gains without pains."
"God helps them that help themselves."

Franklin himself had much in common with middle-
class Americans. The son of a soap and candle maker, he
built his own printing business and even when rich and
famous continued to think of himself as an artisan. Witness the epigraph he wrote for himself:

The body of
B. Franklin, Printer;
(Like the cover of an old book

Its contents worn out
And stripped of its lettering and gilding)
Lies here, food for worms.
But the work shall not be lost;
For it will, (as he believed) appear once more,
In a new and more elegant edition
Revised and corrected
By the Author

Through *Poor Richard's Almanack*, Franklin became, as Nathaniel Hawthorne put it in 1842, "the counselor and household friend to almost every family in America." He was, William Dean Howells wrote in 1888, "the most modern, the most American, of his contemporaries." Franklin personified the American dream, and he celebrated it in the *Almanack* and in his *Autobiography*.

Not surprisingly, those less eager to celebrate the capitalist, materialistic side of America held Franklin in disdain. These included D. H. Lawrence, who in 1923 referred to Franklin as "sound, satisfied Ben," as "this dry, moral, utilitarian little democrat," and as a "virtuous little automaton." Groucho Marx, writing in 1959 but very much in the spirit of Twain, called the "early-to-bed" advice "a lot of hoopla" and noted that most of the wealthy people he knew "will fire the help if they are disturbed before three in the afternoon." In 2000, essayist David Brooks called Franklin "our Founding Yuppie."

None of this was fair to Franklin, who certainly worked and lived for more than money. "I would rather have it said, *He lived usefully*, than, *He died rich*," Franklin wrote to William Strahan in 1750, and Franklin's life was indeed almost inconceivably useful. He served his fellow citizens by, just to name a few of his projects, founding the Library Company of Philadelphia; organizing the city's first fire company; promoting plans to pave, clean, and light the city's streets; establishing an academy that was designed to prepare students for business and public service and that later became the University of Pennsylvania; founding the Pennsylvania Hospital; and presiding over the Pennsylvania Society for Promoting the Abolition of Slavery. That list doesn't include his two areas of greatest service: science and politics.

"Let the experiment be made"

Franklin's inventions included bifocals, a stove for heating that provided more heat and less smoke, and, most famously, the lightning rod.

Franklin made many contributions to the science of electricity, coining terms we still use such as *battery*, *charged*, *neutral*, *condense*, and *conductor*. He also had fun with electricity: he created a leaping metal spider, a picture of King George II that produced a "high-treason" shock when someone touched the crown, and a turkey dinner in which the turkey was killed by an electrical shock. "The birds killed in this manner eat uncommonly tender," he wrote his friend Peter Collinson in 1749.

For Franklin, who was always as interested in the healthy and wealthy as the wise, the question was: was there a useful application of this increased understanding of electricity? The answer was the lightning rod. Like other scientists, Franklin had observed static electricity in an early capacitor known as a Leyden jar, and he knew electricity and lightning had many properties in common. He knew electricity could be drawn off by pointed metal objects, and he suspected this might work for lightning as well.

"Let the experiment be made," he declared.

In 1750, he described his plan to Collinson. "Houses, ships and even towns and churches may be effectually secured from the stroke of lightning by their means," he wrote. "The electrical fire would, I think, be drawn out of a cloud silently."

In the summer of 1752, Franklin launched his kite into the clouds. A sharp wire protruding from the top of the kite attracted lightning, and the string—to Franklin's great satisfaction—drew sparks to a wire near the base of the wet string. The experiment was actually quite dangerous, but it convinced Franklin that if the string could safely guide a current into the ground, so could a metal rod. By that fall, lightning rods were going up on Philadelphia's public buildings and on Franklin's home, and the new edition of *Poor Richard's Almanack* was already advertising them. "It has pleased God in his goodness to mankind, at length to discover to them the means of securing their habitations and other buildings from mischief by thunder and lightning," Franklin wrote in the *Almanack*. Lightning rods soon spread to other colonies and to Europe.

Franklin was, the German philosopher Immanuel Kant said, the "New Prometheus." He had stolen the fire of heaven.

Not everyone was so thrilled. Some argued lightning rods would interfere with the will of God (to which Franklin responded: "Surely the thunder of heaven is no more supernatural than the rain, hail, or sunshine of heaven, against the inconvenience of which we guard by roofs and shades without scruple"). Others, eager to deflate Franklin's reputation, noted that French scientists drew lightning from pointed rods (albeit attached to buildings, not kites) months before Franklin flew his kite. This is true, though Franklin still deserves a great deal of the credit. The French experiments were a direct result of Franklin's letters to Collinson, which were published in England in 1751 and France in 1752. Indeed, King Louis XV, Collinson wrote Franklin, ordered his scientists to perform Franklin's proposed experiment and also ordered them to "convey compliments in an express manner to Mr. Franklin of Philadelphia for the useful discoveries in electricity and application of the pointed rods to prevent the terrible effects of thunderstorms." Moreover, at least according to his own later account, Franklin didn't know about the French successes until after he'd completed his own experiment.

"Join, or Die"

Next, Franklin applied his characteristic pragmatism to politics. The immediate problems were the French and Indians, who in 1754 were attacking British settlements in the Ohio Valley.

Franklin's solution was "A Plan for the Union of all the Colonies," which he drew up en route to Albany, where representatives from each colony would meet to discuss the problem. To illustrate the need for unity, Franklin published in the May 9, 1754, *Pennsylvania Gazette* one of America's earliest political cartoons and perhaps the earliest symbol of a united America. The picture was a severed snake representing the disunited colonies. The caption read: "Join, or Die."

At the Albany conference, Franklin managed to persuade his fellow representatives to accept his plan. That was as far as it went, however. The Albany Plan was quickly rejected both by the British Parliament, which feared a united America might someday turn on Britain instead of the French and Indians, and by the colonies themselves, who distrusted each other as much as they did the British.

"The [colonial] assemblies did not adopt it as they all thought there was too much *prerogative* in it," Franklin later wrote in his autobiography, "and in England it was judged to have too much of the *democratic*."

"Don't tread on me"

The unity Franklin had in mind in 1754 was very much a unity of British colonies, not an independent America. Indeed, Franklin was a devoted royalist who lived most of the following years in London, enjoying his fame, having his portrait painted, and mingling with other famous Englishmen. He used his connections to secure a royal governorship for his son, William, in 1762 and only returned to America that year to carry out his duties as deputy postmaster general, a royal office. His devotion to the British government was somewhat shaken by the 1765 Stamp Act, but he continued to try to bridge the growing gap between the mother country and colonies until 1774. When British officials learned that Franklin had sent to America some old but embarrassing letters of Boston's lieutenant governor Thomas Hutchinson, the government harshly and publicly attacked Franklin, then fired him from his job as deputy postmaster. Humiliated, Franklin returned to America and took up the patriot cause.

Franklin's fellow Americans were also turning against the British. By the end of 1775, Franklin's snake, no longer severed, was transforming itself into a coiled rattlesnake. This image of a united and dangerous America could be seen in December 1775 on a flag flying on an American naval vessel, the *Alfred*, with the snake against a yellow background and above the words "Dont tread on me." It's possible that Franklin suggested using the rattlesnake as a symbol. It was Franklin, after all, who illustrated "Join, or Die" with a disjointed snake, and it was also Franklin who, in 1751, proposed that Americans dump rattlesnakes in St. James Square in retaliation for the British having sent convicts to Pennsylvania.

Most historians, however, credit the image and words to Christopher Gadsden, a leading South Carolina patriot and a member of the Continental Congress. The evidence for Gadsden is circumstantial but substantial. Gadsden was a leading advocate of an American navy and a member of a committee Congress appointed to create one. He grew up in South Carolina's lowcountry, where he would have learned to respect rattlesnakes. And Gadsden clearly liked the flag very much, since in February 1776, according to the records of the South Carolina provincial Congress, he presented to the legislature "an elegant standard, such as is to be used by the Commander-in-Chief of the American Navy, being a yellow field, with a lively representation of a rattlesnake in the middle, in the attitude of going to strike, and these words underneath, 'Don't tread on me!'"

The rattlesnake and its accompanying motto were extremely popular during the Revolution. In the late twentieth and early twenty-first centuries, the Gadsden flag was adopted by libertarians.

"We must . . . all hang together, or most assuredly we shall all hang separately"

The most famous words to come out of the Revolution were those in the Declaration of Independence, and Thomas Jefferson surely deserves the credit for them. Franklin's edits of the Declaration along with those of John Adams and other members of the Congress, however, were by no means insignificant.

In Jefferson's first draft, he declared: "We hold these truths to be sacred and undeniable." Franklin took his black printer's pen, crossed out "sacred and undeniable," and made the phrase: "We hold these truths to be self-evident." In using the word "sacred," Jefferson had—perhaps unintentionally—tied the equality of all men and their inalienable rights to religion. "Franklin's edit," wrote his biographer Walter Isaacson, "turned it instead into an assertion of rationality."

Franklin's contributions to independence went well beyond editing. Once he committed to the cause, he was one of its strongest advocates, pushing the delegates toward a united stand. "He does not hesitate at our boldest measures," Adams wrote to his wife, Abigail, in July 1775, "but rather seems to think us too irresolute."

Franklin's most famous declaration of unity came at the official signing of the Declaration. "There must be no pulling different ways," said John Hancock, the president of the Continental Congress, as he put his oversized signature on the document. "We must all hang together."

"Yes, we must, indeed, all hang together," Franklin added, "or most assuredly we shall all hang separately."

These particular words first appeared in Jared Sparks's 1840 edition of Franklin's works, so again there have been debunkers who have argued Franklin never said them. The fact that there's no contemporary account of the anecdote and that Sparks introduces it merely as "another anecdote related of Franklin" must indeed make one skeptical. Still, it sure sounds like Franklin, who loved to pun and who saw in the most somber of moments an opportunity for a punch line.

Soon after the Declaration was signed, Franklin was sent to France to secure another form of unity: an alliance with France. He was already well known there from his visits during his long stays in London; indeed, he was a celebrity there because of his experiments (Marie Antoinette referred to him as "l'Ambassadeur Electrique"). Now the American ambassador, he became a symbol of America. Amid the glamour of Louis XVI's court, Franklin insisted on dressing in plain white and brown linen, almost always with a fur cap on his head. Franklin used all this to his—and America's—advantage, charming the king and his ministers and securing the French alliance.

Adams, who arrived in Paris in 1778 to join the negotiations only to find Franklin had already concluded them, could not hide his jealousy. "His reputation was more universal than that of Leibnitz or Newton, Frederick [the Great] or Voltaire, and his character more beloved and esteemed than any or all of them," Adams grumbled in his diary. "His name was familiar to government and people, to kings, courtiers, nobility, clergy, and philosophers, as well as plebeians, to such a degree that there was scarcely a peasant or a citizen, a valet de chamber, coachman or footman, a lady's chambermaid or a scullion in a kitchen, who was not familiar with it, and who did not consider him as a friend to human kind."

Less resentfully, the French finance minister Anne-Robert-Jacques Turgot summed up Franklin this way: "He snatched the lightning from the skies and the scepter from the tyrants."

"A republic if you can keep it"

Franklin's final efforts on behalf of American unity came at the Constitutional Convention of 1787, where he negotiated a crucial compromise between large and small states. The deal was that the states would be represented equally in the Senate and in proportion to their populations in the House of Representatives.

Roger Sherman, not Franklin, was the first to suggest the compromise, and Franklin did not particularly like the idea. He correctly saw something undemocratic in giving senators from Rhode Island or Delaware the same amount of power as those from Virginia or Pennsylvania. Yet Franklin also saw that without compromise there would be no Constitution—and no United States of America—so he threw his considerable influence behind the deal.

At eighty-one, by far the oldest of the delegates, Franklin sometimes had to give his speeches to other delegates to read, but the words were undeniably his.

"Both sides must part with some of their demands," he told his fellow delegates. "We are sent hither to *consult*, not to *contend*, with each other."

Franklin remained silent as the Convention reached another crucial compromise whereby slaves would be counted, for the purpose of apportioning votes in the House of Representatives, as three-fifths of a person. His silence may have reflected a lack of resolve: though he was by 1787 a committed abolitionist, Franklin continued to own slaves until his death. Most likely, though, it was another example of his belief that, without compromise, there would be no Constitution.

"I consent, sir, to this constitution because I expect no better, and because I am not sure that it is not the best," Franklin said in his closing speech at the Convention. "I cannot help expressing a wish that every member of the convention who may still have objections to it, would, with me, on this occasion, doubt a little of his own infallibility."

After the delegates voted in favor of the Constitution, they filed out into the hall. The document would not go into effect until nine of the thirteen states ratified it, but the Convention had created a new government. According to James McHenry, a delegate from Maryland who kept a journal, a woman named Mrs. Powel approached Franklin and asked him what kind of government it would be. "A republic," Franklin answered, "if you can keep it."

Chapter 7

Nathan Hale

"I only regret that I have but one life to lose for my country"

IN THE SUMMER of 1776, George Washington's troops were holed up in Manhattan while a significantly bigger and better-supplied British force massed across the East River in Brooklyn. Desperate to know the British plans, Washington asked for a volunteer to go behind enemy lines. Up stepped Captain Nathan Hale.

Hale was remarkably unqualified to be a spy. He had graduated from Yale, then had become a schoolteacher. Now he was a member of a special corps commanded by Lieutenant Colonel Thomas Knowlton and known as Knowlton's Rangers. The rangers essentially acted as scouts for Washington.

Unlike scouting, however, spying required trickery, and this was a skill Hale sorely lacked. His fellow officer and good friend Captain William Hull, in a memoir published in 1848, recalled of Hale that "his nature was too frank and open for deceit and disguise, and he was incapable of acting a part equally foreign to his feelings and habits."

Hull tried to dissuade Hale from taking the assignment by arguing that spying was dishonorable. "Every kind of service, necessary to the public good, becomes honorable by being necessary," Hale told Hull.

Hull tried to make clear the danger. "I am fully sensible of the consequences of discovery and capture in such a situation," Hale replied (this still according to the 1848 Hull memoir). "But for a year I have been attached to the army and have not rendered any material service. . . . I wish to be useful."

So, on September 15th, Hale sailed across Long Island Sound, landing about fifty miles east of the British camp. He donned a brown suit and a broad-brimmed hat suitable for the schoolmaster he was pretending to be. About the same time Hale arrived in Long Island, British General William Howe led his troops across the East River and seized Manhattan.

This made Hale's position not only dangerous but also pointless. Still, he headed toward Brooklyn, figuring he might learn something along the way. Behind British lines this Yankee was, alas, as out of place as Mark Twain's Connecticut Yankee in King Arthur's court—and as easily spotted. By some accounts, Hale was betrayed by a Tory cousin, but more likely it was Hale's own actions that raised British suspicions. He was arrested September 21st.

There was no trial. Howe, in the midst of a major campaign, had neither the time nor the interest. Besides, there was no doubt Hale was guilty: he had admitted he was an officer in the Continental army, he was wearing civilian clothes behind British lines, and he was caught with various incriminating documents in his possession. Faced with overwhelming evidence, Hale confessed. Howe ordered that he be hanged, and the next day he was.

Exactly where Hale died has been the subject of some contention. It was first thought to be somewhere downtown. Most historians now think it was east of what's now Central Park.

Far more contentious are Hale's last words. The version in the 1848 Hull memoirs—"I only regret, that I have but one life to lose for my country"—has (minus a comma) become the best-known one, as much a part of patriotic lore as Patrick Henry's liberty or death. Yet it is at best secondhand; Hull, an American officer, certainly wasn't present at a British execution. The only firsthand account we have of Hale's death is from British Captain Frederick MacKenzie. In a September 22nd diary entry, MacKenzie wrote: "He behaved with great composure and resolution, saying he thought it the duty of every good officer, to obey any orders given him by his commander in chief; and desired the spectators to be at all times prepared to meet death in whatever shape it might appear."

A version more like Hull's appeared in print in 1777, when the *Essex Journal* of Newburyport, Massachusetts, reported that Hale, at the scaffold, said that "if he had ten thousand lives, he would lay them all down, if called to it, in defence of his injured, bleeding country." No source is given, though some historians think it may have been Hull. Four years later the Boston *Independent Chronicle* quoted Hale thusly: "I am so satisfied with the cause in which I have engaged, that my only regret is, that I have not more lives than one to offer in its service."

Still, to be mentioned in a couple of newspapers was hardly acclaim worthy of a great hero of the Revolution. Indeed, Major John Andre, a British spy implicated in Benedict Arnold's treachery and executed in 1780, generated far more attention from his contemporaries, American as well as British. In two of the earliest histories of the Revolution—William Gordon's 1788 *History of the Rise, Progress, and Establishment of the Independence of the United States of America* and David Ramsay's 1789 *History of the American Revolution*—there was plenty about Andre but no mention of Hale.

Hale finally moved onto center stage in Hannah Adams's 1799 *Summary History of New England and General Sketch of the American War*. Adams praised Hale as Andre's superior. Crediting Hull, she concluded her account of

Hale's death as follows: "Unknown to all around him, without a single friend to offer him the least consolation, thus fell as amiable and as worthy a young man as America could boast, with this, as his dying observation, 'that he only lamented that he had but one life to lose for his country.'" Hale's death also appeared in Jedediah Morse's 1824 *Annals of the American Revolution*.

By now, Hale was more generally hailed as a hero, and his old acquaintances were weighing in with accounts of his life and death. In 1837, the Missouri *Republic* published a letter from Stephen Hempstead, the sergeant who had ferried Hale across Long Island Sound never to see him again. "He died upon the 'inglorious tree,'" Hempstead wrote, "not the death of a soldier, but . . . for his country's sake."

Finally, in 1848, Hull's memoirs appeared, albeit twenty-three years after Hull's death and edited, if not written in large part, by Hull's daughter. Here Hull (or his daughter) has settled on dying words considerably pithier than earlier versions and just as we remember them today.

The 1848 memoir also explained how Hull learned about Hale's final moments. Sometime after Hale's death, Captain John Montresor, a British officer, visited Washington's camp to discuss a prisoner exchange. There he met Hull and described Hale's death.

"On the morning of his execution," Montresor told Hull, "my station was near the fatal spot. . . . Captain Hale entered: he was calm, and bore himself with gentle dignity, in the consciousness of rectitude and high intentions."

Montresor, according to the 1848 Hull memoir, continued: "But a few persons were around him, yet his characteristic dying words were remembered. He said, 'I only regret, that I have but one life to lose for my country.'"

Whatever Hale said, he was probably paraphrasing. He may have been familiar with the words of John Lilburne, a seventeenth-century leader of a radical British democratic group known as Levelers. At one of his many trials, Lilburne said: "I am sorry I have but one life to lose, in maintaining the truth, justice, and righteousness, of so gallant a piece." Another time, Lilburne declared that, "if I had a million of lives, I would sacrifice them all against you."

And Hale, as a Yale graduate and schoolteacher, was almost certainly familiar with Joseph Addison's then-famous play *Cato*. In Addison's version, the Roman politician Cato, on seeing the body of his son Marcus, laments:

How beautiful is death when earned by virtue!
Who would not be that youth? What pity it is
That we can die but once to serve our country!

CHAPTER 8

ALEXANDER HAMILTON

"I never expect to see a perfect work from imperfect man"

WE KNOW him best as the face on the ten dollar bill. Rightly so, for of all the founders it was Alexander Hamilton who did the most to set the nation's economy on a firm basis. If Thomas Jefferson set forth the nation's ideals, Hamilton established its reality: an economy ruled not by planters but by traders and bankers; a professional military; a powerful chief executive. As the nation's first secretary of the treasury, Hamilton created a budget system, a tax system, a funded debt, a central bank, and a customs service.

This was no way to win the hearts of future generations. "We're still Jefferson's children," proclaimed Ronald Reagan in 1987. Hamilton, in contrast, was in Noah Webster's words "the evil genius of this country" or in Woodrow Wilson's somewhat more generous estimate, "a very great man, but not a great American." By the end of the New Deal, Hamilton was considered, as historian Stephen Knott put it, "something akin to a hybrid mix of Ebenezer Scrooge and Benito Mussolini." His image has improved in recent years, but there is little likelihood that a Hamilton Memorial will ever be built on the Mall in Washington.

There is no doubt, however, that Hamilton's words were among the most influential of any American's. Above all, there were the words of *The Federalist*, a series of eighty-five essays written in 1787 and 1788 to build support for the Constitution just drafted in Philadelphia. James Madison and John Jay wrote some of these, but it was Hamilton who conceived the project, talked Madison and Jay into collaborating, arranged the publication, and wrote fifty-one of the essays himself. What Hamilton had to overcome, through *The Federalist*, was a deep-seated distrust of the proposed constitution's strong central government. Would not this constitution, the anti-Federalists argued at the Constitutional Convention and then in essays of their own, create a government much like that against which Americans had just rebelled? Patrick Henry was among those who compared "the tyranny of Philadelphia" to "the tyranny of George III."

The Federalist is generally recognized as a masterpiece, all the more remarkable for having been written under the pressure of newspaper deadlines. Theodore Roosevelt called it "on the whole the greatest book" about politics. Jay, who because of illness wrote only five essays, covered foreign relations. Madison surveyed the history of republics. Hamilton, ever practical, focused on the government's machinery, particularly that of the executive branch.

Directly countering the anti-Federalists, he declared, "Energy in the executive is a leading character in the definition of good government." As for the dangers, these were exaggerated: the president, unlike a British king, did not have an absolute veto over legislation, nor could he dissolve the Congress or declare war or make treaties.

The Constitution might not be perfect, he conceded, but it was as good a plan as possible, and far better than the alternatives. After all, wrote Hamilton in the last of *The Federalist* essays, "I never expect to see a perfect work from imperfect man."

"Your people is a great beast"

As the first secretary of the treasury, Hamilton went from talking about the power of the presidency to exercising and expanding that power. He pushed, for example, for a national bank and a system of taxation that would allow the federal government to assume and pay the debts of the states. To his critics, Hamilton came to represent a government as dangerous to their liberty as that of Great Britain.

Over and over, his critics turned Hamilton's words against him. "In his private opinion," wrote Madison, whose alliance with Hamilton did not long outlast *The Federalist*, "he had no scruple in declaring . . . that the British Gov[ernmen]t was the best in the world and that he doubted much whether anything short of it would do in America."

It was Jefferson who became Hamilton's most vehement critic. Hamilton "was not only a monarchist, but for a monarchy bottomed on corruption," Jefferson wrote in the *Anas*, a collection of political reminiscences he put together in 1818. He told of a dinner he and Adams and Hamilton had shared in 1791. The subject of conversation was the British political system.

"Purge that constitution of its corruption . . . and it would be the most perfect constitution ever devised by the wit of man," said Adams. To which Hamilton responded: "Purge it of its corruption . . . and it would become an impracticable government: as it stands, with all its supposed defects, it is the most perfect government which ever existed."

Another anecdote Jefferson often repeated cast Hamilton in an even worse light. In 1791, Hamilton visited Jefferson at the latter's lodging in Philadelphia and asked about the three portraits on the wall. Jefferson explained they were "the three greatest men the world has ever produced . . . Sir Francis Bacon, Sir Isaac Newton, and John Locke." Hamilton supposedly replied, "The greatest man that ever lived was Julius Caesar."

To Jefferson, stories like these proved Hamilton was at heart a monarchist and a would-be tyrant. Jefferson's stories, however, lacked context. Hamilton undoubtedly did defend aspects of the British system, but so did many others; until the Revolution, Americans had demanded not independence from Britain but their rights as British citizens. It was only seven months before the Declaration of Independence that Jefferson himself wrote that "there is not in the British empire a man who more cordially loves a union with Great Britain than I do."

As time passed and America seemed less likely to become a monarchy, the attacks on Hamilton focused less on his alleged monarchism and more on his alleged regard for the rich and disregard for the public in general. Hamilton's support for a national bank fed these suspicions. "I have ever been the enemy of banks," Jefferson wrote Adams, adding that they were "seeking to filch from the public their swindling, and barren gains."

Of all the stories about Hamilton, perhaps the most damaging appeared first in the memoirs of Theophilus Parsons, who was attorney general under John Adams. The setting is another dinner party, again soon after the Constitution was adopted. As a guest exulted over the wisdom of the American people, Hamilton—according to Parsons—pounded on the table and cried out, "Your people, sir—your people is a great beast!" The story was at best secondhand, however, and many historians have questioned whether Hamilton actually uttered these words.

Certainly Hamilton always claimed he was a loyal supporter of the republic. He had fought in the Revolution, leading a charge on a British stronghold during the siege of Yorktown; he had fought for the Constitution in *The Federalist*. "I am affectionately attached to the republican theory," he insisted to Edward Carrington in a 1792 letter. "I desire above all things to see the equality of political rights, exclusive of all hereditary distinction, firmly established." Jefferson was a "contemptible hypocrite," a man who talked about liberty while accumulating power, not to mention slaves.

To hear our founding fathers attack each other—essentially accusing each other of betraying the Revolution—is to see them in an unflattering light. Men whom we think of as brilliant, courageous, selfless, and united come across as jealous and vindictive. Partly this is because they were human—and flawed. The politics of the period were every bit as vicious as American politics in any period since. Occasionally, it even became violent: witness Hamilton's death in 1804 in a duel with Aaron Burr, who was Jefferson's vice president. Yet the viciousness of their politics also drives home how much was at stake. The Revolution formally ended in 1783 with the signing of the Treaty of Paris. But the nature of the American democracy—indeed, its very survival—had not yet been determined. Hamilton understood this; so did Jefferson and Madison and Adams, and the intensity of their words grew out of their genuine belief that the fate of the republic was in their hands.

As for Hamilton's loyalty to American ideals, it's worth noting that Washington, despite constant complaints from Jefferson, never backed away from his secretary of the treasury. "By some he is considered as an ambitious man, and therefore a dangerous one," Washington wrote in 1798. "That he is ambitious I shall readily grant; but it is of that laudable kind which prompts a man to excel in whatever he takes in hand."

CHAPTER 9

JOHN HANCOCK

"I write so that King George III may read without his spectacles"

HE WAS AN unlikely revolutionary. John Hancock inherited one of America's largest commercial enterprises—its operations included retailing, wholesaling, importing and exporting, warehouses, ships and wharfs, banking, and real estate—and he enjoyed his wealth immensely. He lived in a mansion atop Boston's Beacon Hill. When he descended from the hill (all of which he owned), it was in a gilded coach with the Hancock coat of arms on its doors. He wore fashionable wigs, clothes of silk and velvet, shoes with silver and gold buckles.

Yet a revolutionary he most surely was. At first, like other colonists, Hancock hoped for reconciliation with Great Britain. When Parliament passed the Stamp Act, Hancock wrote his London agent: "We are not able to bear all things . . . these taxes will greatly affect us, our trade will be ruined." Politics was not yet his highest priority, however, and he made sure to let his agent know he needed "two pipes [about 125 gallons each] of the very best Madeira for my own table." Added Hancock: "I don't stand at any price, let it be good, I like rich wine."

He moved closer to rebellion in 1768 when the crew of one his ships, the *Liberty*, attempted to sneak a cargo of wine into Boston. Customs officials seized the *Liberty* and charged Hancock with tax evasion. Lacking any witnesses willing to testify, British authorities eventually dropped the charges, but the process turned Hancock, in the mind of the public, from foppish aristocrat to champion of colonial rights. By 1774, he was among the Revolutionary leaders who addressed a huge crowd on the anniversary of the Boston Massacre. He urged Massachusetts towns to organize militias and prepare to fight the British, or, as he called them, "bloody butchers," "dark designing knaves," and "murderers."

In 1775, Massachusetts chose Hancock as a delegate to the Continental Congress. When Peyton Randolph, the president of the Congress, returned to Virginia, the Congress elected Hancock to take his place. A few of the more radical patriots, such as Samuel Adams, complained about Hancock's "unrepublican ostentation." Others, including John Adams, grumbled about the "impropriety" of Hancock continuing as president when Randolph returned from Virginia, but that awkwardness dissipated when Randolph, soon after, died. Overall, though, Hancock's appointment made political sense. Coming from Boston, that center of anti-British fervor, Hancock appealed to most of the radicals in Congress. At the same time, his wealth and aristocratic manner reassured plantation owners from the South.

The following months attested to the wisdom of the delegates' decision. Hancock presided over the debates evenhandedly, keeping both sides cool through the heat of a Philadelphia summer and gently pushing his more conservative colleagues toward independence. Most delegates agreed with Virginian Benjamin Harrison, who called Hancock "noble" and "generous." And later none could deny that Hancock, perhaps more than any other delegate, put his own fortune on the line by spending over the course of the Revolution about one hundred thousand pounds of his own money on arms and ammunitions for George Washington's army.

The moment for which Hancock is best remembered came after the delegates adopted the Declaration of Independence. As president of Congress—and in a sense, therefore, president of the United States—it was Hancock who first signed the Declaration. Hancock put his famous signature on the paper in handwriting twice as large as any other signer's and with a flourish underneath. "I write," he explained, "so that King George III may read without his spectacles." One by one, the other members of Congress then solemnly approached the table on which the document sat and added their own signatures.

Or so the story goes.

Whether Hancock actually said these words is highly questionable. The earliest printed version appears in John F. Watson's 1857 *Annals of Philadelphia and Pennsylvania in the Olden Time*. According to Watson, after signing the Declaration Hancock rose from his seat and said, "There! John Bull can read my name without spectacles, and may now double his reward of 500 pounds for my head." (John Bull was not the king but a symbol of the nation—sort of a British version of Uncle Sam.) Watson offered no reference, and the words were presumably by then already part of American folklore.

Perhaps more shocking to most Americans is that the members of Congress did not sign the Declaration on July 4th. True, John Adams, Benjamin Franklin, and Thomas Jefferson—the first two of whom were on the committee to draft the document and the third of whom wrote most of the draft—all later recalled the signing taking place on the fourth. Adams and Franklin mentioned the date in letters years later, and Jefferson wrote in his *Autobiography*: "The debates having taken up the greater part of the 2d, 3d, and 4th days of July were in the evening of the

last closed, the declaration was reported by the committee, agreed to by the House and signed by every member
present except Mr. Dickinson."

Yet almost all historians who have studied the matter
believe Adams, Franklin, and Jefferson were mistaken. Historians pored over the original manuscript minutes of the
journals of Congress and found no mention of a signing on
the Fourth. No signed copy of the Declaration dated July
4th exists, nor is there a contemporary letter stating it was
signed that day. Julian Boyd, the editor of Jefferson's papers,
argued that when it came to the history of the Declaration
of Independence "no one was more acutely interested than
Jefferson [and] his testimony should not be discarded." But
even Boyd conceded that there was "all but overwhelming
proof that Jefferson was mistaken."

What did happen on the fourth was that Congress finished revising the Declaration and officially adopted it. On
July 5th, a printed version of the approved Declaration was
inserted in the Congressional journal for the fourth of July.
The text was followed by the words "signed by order and
in behalf of the Congress, John Hancock, President." Congress' secretary, Charles Thomson, also signed the document. Also on July 5th, printed copies were sent to various
state assemblies and conventions as well as military commanders. After all thirteen colonies gave their approval,
Congress ordered an official copy prepared, and finally, on
August 2nd, according to the Congressional journal entry
for that day, the declaration was signed. Hancock was the
first to sign. Fifty-six others followed, though not all signed
that day. A few who were there on July 4th never signed,
including John Dickinson (as Jefferson recalled) and Robert
Livingston (who along with Adams, Franklin, Jefferson, and
Roger Sherman was a member of the committee that
drafted the Declaration).

Hancock, then, fully deserves his place in the story of the Declaration, even if he never said anything about King George or spectacles. His signature on August 2nd was bold and central. And for almost a month after July 4th, the only two signatures on the Declaration were those of Hancock and Thomson. If during July 1776 the British had captured the leaders of the Revolution, it was Hancock whose treason they could most easily have proven, and it was Hancock who would have been the first to hang.

CHAPTER 10

PATRICK HENRY

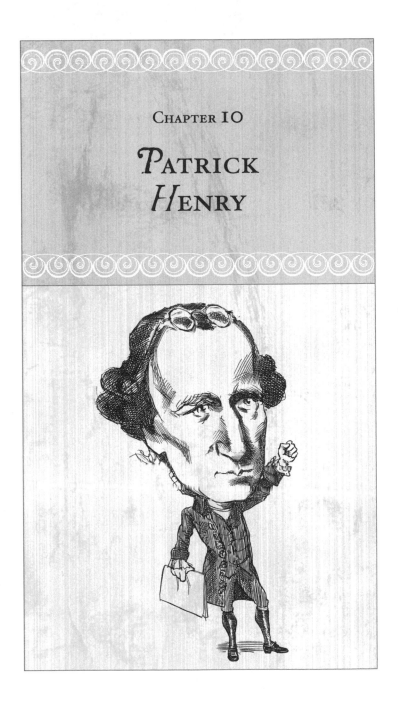

"If this be treason,
make the most of it"

THE STAMP ACT, which became law in March 1765, required colonists to affix stamps to various legal and other papers. To Parliament, the stamps seemed a reasonable way to pay for the 7,500 or so British troops stationed in America. The troops, after all, were there to protect the colonists from the French and the Indians and to administer the territory France ceded at the end of the French and Indian War. To the colonists, at least the more inflamed among them, the act trampled on one of their most fundamental rights: that only their own elected assemblies could tax them.

In May, the twenty-nine-year-old Patrick Henry addressed the Virginia House of Burgesses. Here's how William Wirt described the scene in his biography of Henry, first published in 1817:

> He exclaimed in a voice of thunder, and with the look of a god: "Cesar had his Brutus — Charles the First, his Cromwell — and George the Third — ('Treason!' cried the speaker—Treason, treason! Echoed from every part of the house. . . . Henry faltered not for an instant; but rising to a loftier attitude, and fixing on the speaker an eye of the most determined fire, he finished his sentence with the firmest emphasis) — may profit by their example. If this be treason, make the most of it."

One eyewitness quoted by Wirt was a young student of law, Thomas Jefferson. "I well remember the cry of treason," Jefferson told Wirt, "the pause of Mr. Henry at the name of George III, and the presence of mind with which he closed his sentence, and baffled the charge vociferated."

Henry's words stirred the Burgesses to pass resolutions strongly condemning the act of Parliament, and they opened a chasm between the colonies and Britain. As Wirt put it, Henry's "light and heat were seen and felt throughout the continent; and he was every where regarded as the great champion of colonial liberty. . . . The spirit of resistance became bolder and bolder, until the whole continent was in a flame."

This was not the first time Henry's words had prompted cries of treason. Two years earlier, the young attorney defended the Fredericksville Parish vestry in a case that challenged a tax put into effect by the Burgesses without approval of the Crown. Henry's words then foreshadowed not only his own later comments on tyranny but other colonists' demands of "no taxation without representation." Henry's pleas to the jury, eyewitness William Robinson recalled, horrified "the more sober and virtuous part of the audience . . . some of whom did murmur at the time, 'treason! treason!'"

Yet despite the fame of Henry's 1765 response to the cries of treason, it's by no means clear he ever suggested making the most of it. Wirt's recollections were compiled decades after the event. An anonymous Frenchman whose report was written just one day after the speech and whose journal surfaced in 1921 tells a different story, one in which Henry, confronted with the accusations of treason, immediately apologized to his audience and pledged his loyalty to the king.

"I was entertained with very strong debates concerning duties that the Parliament wants to lay on the American colonies, which they call or style Stamp Duties," the Frenchman wrote.

> Shortly after I came in, one of the members stood up and said he had read in former times Tarquin and Julus had their Brutus, Charles had his Cromwell, and he did not doubt but some good American would stand up, in favour of his country, but (says he) in a more moderate manner, and was going to continue, when the speaker of the house rose and said, he, the last that stood up had spoken treason, and was sorry to see that not one of the members of the house was loyal enough to stop him, before he had gone so far.

So far, the Frenchman's story largely matched the traditional version. But then: "Upon which the same member stood up again (his name is henery)," the Frenchman continued, "and said that if he had affronted the speaker, or the house, he was ready to ask pardon, and he would show his loyalty to his majesty King G. the third, at the expence of the last drop of his blood." Far from challenging the king, here Henry is quickly backpedaling, recognizing that he has gone too far.

Was Wirt's account, then, no different from those of Parson Weems, the biographer of George Washington who invented the story of his chopping down the cherry tree? By no means. Unlike Weems, Wirt drew on the reminiscences of witnesses. Still, Wirt depended on memories clouded by time and myth, and he clearly favored tales that buttressed Henry's status as a patriotic icon. Henry's speech "seized the pillars of the temple, shook them terribly, and seemed to threaten his opponents with ruin. . . . The fainthearted gathered courage . . . and cowards became heroes, while they gazed upon his exploits."

If Wirt mythologized Henry's words, he did not exaggerate their effect. The words did indeed give courage to the fainthearted. In Williamsburg, an angry crowd forced the newly appointed stamp collector to resign. Even moderate leaders like Washington were soon describing the tax as "a direful attack on . . . liberties." Various versions of the resolutions, including one the Burgesses rescinded and two others they never passed, found their way into newspapers in other colonies where they spurred defiance of the Stamp Act. Virginia's resolves, wrote Governor Francis Bernard of Massachusetts, were an "alarm bell to the disaffected." Americans stopped buying British goods, and British merchants pressured Parliament to repeal the tax.

"Give me liberty, or give me death"

Ten years later, the talk among the more radical colonial leaders had shifted from economic to military resistance. When the Second Virginia Convention convened, it did so upriver from the capital, since many of the delegates feared the royal governor, Lord Dunmore, might try to break up the proceedings. Richmond was at the time only a village, with no government building large enough to accommodate the convention, so the delegates assembled at Henrico Parish Church, later named St. John's Church.

On March 23, 1775, Henry put forward a resolution that the colony immediately be put in a "state of defence." More moderate delegates objected, arguing that military preparations would undercut any hope of reconciling with Great Britain. Again, Henry rose to speak, and again we turn to Wirt for his words:

"Gentlemen may cry peace, peace—but there is no peace. The war is actually begun! The next gale that sweeps the north will bring to our ears the clash of resounding arms! Our brethren are already in the field! Why stand we here idle? What is it that gentlemen wish? What would they have? Is life so dear, or peace so sweet, as to be purchased at the price of chains and slavery? Forbid it, Almighty God! I know not what course others may take; but as for me," cried he, with both his arms extended aloft, his brows knit, every feature marked with the resolute purpose of his soul, and his voice swelled to its boldest note of exclamation—"give me liberty, or give me death!"

Without any contemporary record of Henry's words, it is impossible to know how many of these were Henry's and how many were Wirt's. Some of the words may even have been drawn from Joseph Addison's 1713 play, *Cato*. Wrote Addison: "The hand of fate is over us, and heav'n / Exacts severity from all our thoughts: / It is not now a time to talk of aught / But chains, or conquest; liberty or death."

For the Liberty or Death speech, Wirt named two sources: St. George Tucker and John Tyler, both of whom were present at St John's Church. Others who were there (including Jefferson) did not contradict Wirt's account (though Jefferson did say Wirt's was "a poor book, written in bad taste, and gives an imperfect idea of Patrick Henry"). It seems likely, therefore, that the general outline of the speech and at least some of the words were Henry's.

Whatever the exact words, there can again be no doubt of their impact. According to Edmund Randolph, the convention sat in silence for several minutes. Thomas Marshall told his son John, who later became chief justice of the

Supreme Court, that the speech was "one of the most bold, vehement, and animated pieces of eloquence that had ever been delivered." Edward Carrington, who was listening outside a window of the church, asked to be buried at this spot. In 1810, he got his wish.

More immediately, Henry's resolution passed, and Henry was named chairman of the committee assigned to build a militia. Dunmore reacted by seizing the gunpowder in the public magazine at Williamsburg, Virginia's equivalent of the battles of Lexington and Concord.

"Every word he says not only engages but commands the attention," said George Mason on hearing Henry speak, "and your passions are no longer your own when he addresses them."

"Scholars, understandably, are troubled by the way Wirt brought into print Henry's classic Liberty or Death speech," wrote historian Bernard Mayo. "Yet . . . its expressions . . . seemed to have burned themselves into men's memories. Certainly its spirit is that of the fiery orator who in 1775 so powerfully influenced Virginians and events leading to American independence."

Chapter II

Thomas Jefferson

"We hold these truths to be self-evident"

ON JUNE 7, 1776, Richard Henry Lee, following the instructions of the Virginia Convention, introduced a resolution at the Continental Congress in Philadelphia "that these United colonies are, and of right ought to be, free and independent States, that they are absolved from all allegiance to the British Crown, and that all political connection between them and the State of Great Britain is, and ought to be, totally dissolved." The Continental Congress adopted Lee's resolution and then appointed a committee of five—John Adams, Benjamin Franklin, Roger Sherman, Thomas Jefferson, and Robert Livingston—to turn the resolution into a declaration of independence. Adams took charge and promptly assigned Jefferson to write a draft.

Jefferson did not want to do it. He watched Lee depart for home and longed to follow him. He was convinced that what was going on in Williamsburg, where the Convention's delegates were drafting a constitution for the newly independent commonwealth, mattered more than what was going on in Philadelphia. Jefferson had even written a draft constitution that he hoped the Convention would adopt. What was the point of independence if you didn't create the right form of government? "Should a bad government be instituted for us in the future," he wrote Thomas Nelson in May 1776, "it had been as well to have accepted at first the bad one offered to us from beyond the water without the risk and expense of contest."

Jefferson suggested Adams should draft the Declaration himself. Adams declined, giving several reasons, which he repeated years later in his autobiography:

1. That he was a Virginian and I a Massachusettensian.
2. That he was a southern man and I a northern one.
3. That I had been so obnoxious for my early and constant zeal in promoting the measure, that any draft of mine, would undergo a more severe scrutiny and criticism in Congress, than one of his composition. 4thly and lastly that would be reason enough if there were no other, I had a great opinion of the elegance of his pen and none at all of my own.

Adams's arguments, Jefferson had to admit, made sense. Jefferson went to work and, a day or two later, produced a draft of what would become the Declaration of Independence.

How he managed to write, in a matter of a day or two, the words that more than any others made America has been the subject of much debate. Part of the answer is he didn't start from scratch. He had with him in Philadelphia, and he clearly drew from, his own previous writings, including his 1774 *Summary View of the Rights of British America*, his 1775 "Declaration . . . Setting forth the Causes and Necessity of their taking up Arms," and his draft of a constitution for Virginia. He also had others' recent works at hand, most notably a draft of Virginia's Declaration of Rights, which was written by George Mason and adopted with amendments in the Virginia Convention. Mason's declaration opened by stating: "That all men are born equally free and independent, and have certain inherent natural rights, of which they cannot, by any compact, deprive or divest their posterity; among which are the enjoyment of life and liberty, with the means of acquiring and possessing property, and pursuing and obtaining happiness and safety." Jefferson's most famous words were clearly derived from Mason's; in Jefferson's rough draft of the Declaration, men were "created equal," they had "rights inherent and inalienable" (which he later changed to "inherent and inalienable rights"), and these rights included "the preservation of life, and liberty, and the pursuit of happiness" (which he later changed to "life, liberty, and the pursuit of happiness").

Jefferson also drew from works that he did not have at his side in Philadelphia. He was familiar with the writings of seventeenth-century English writers, including John Milton, Algernon Sidney, and above all John Locke, who set forth a doctrine of natural rights in his *Second Treatise on Government*. He may also have drawn from Scottish philosophers, especially Francis Hutcheson.

Jefferson submitted his draft to Adams and Franklin, who made a few changes, among them that the rights Jefferson had declared to be "sacred and undeniable" were instead "self-evident." The committee then sent the document on to the Congress, which made a total of eighty-six changes. Most involved cutting (about a quarter of Jefferson's text was eliminated), but the Congress also played with Jefferson's language, for example changing "inherent and inalienable rights" to "certain inalienable rights." "Inalienable" later became "unalienable," probably when the Declaration was printed (the latter was more customary in the eighteenth century). Thus the words in their most familiar form: "We hold these truths to be self-evident, that all men are created equal, that they are endowed by their Creator with certain unalienable rights, that among these are life, liberty and the pursuit of happiness."

For Jefferson, seeing his words changed was agonizing, and some others also questioned the results. Richard Henry Lee wrote Jefferson that he wished "that the manuscript had not been mangled as it is." Franklin, Jefferson later recalled, "perceived that I was not insensible to these mutilations" and tried to console him by telling him a story about a hatter who wrote what he considered superb copy for a sign advertising his store, then watched his friends edit it down to simply his name and a picture of a hat. Jefferson's hat, this mangled manuscript, contained words that more than any made America; as Jefferson himself put it in 1824, the Declaration was "the signal of arousing men to burst the chains under which monkish ignorance and superstition had persuaded them to bind themselves."

But—with so many sources and so many editors—was the Declaration truly Jefferson's?

Adams, who was admittedly jealous of Jefferson, later wrote that there was "not an idea in it, but what had been hackneyed in Congress for two years before." Jefferson denied he had copied any other writing: "I turned to neither book nor pamphlet while writing it," he insisted in an 1823 letter to James Madison. Jefferson did not deny, however, that the words of others, past and present, were on his mind. Indeed, it would hardly have been possible to secure Congress's support for independence had Jefferson's words not been, as he put it in an 1825 letter to Henry Lee, "an expression of the American mind." His purpose, he explained to Lee, had been "not to find out new principles, or new arguments, never before thought of, not merely to say things which had never been said before; but to place before mankind the common sense of the subject, in terms so plain and firm as to command their assent." The Declaration's authority, Jefferson rightly added, "rests . . . on the harmonizing sentiments of the day, whether expressed in conversation, in letters, printed essays, or the elementary books of public right, as Aristotle, Cicero, Locke, Sidney, etc."

By the 1820s, when Jefferson rose to defend his authorship, the Declaration was well on its way to becoming the premiere "expression of the American mind." Partly, this was because of partisan politics. When Jefferson emerged as the leader of the Republican Party, his supporters began to celebrate the "deathless instrument" penned by "the immortal Jefferson." Jefferson's opponents in the Federalist Party argued that he wrote only a "small part of that memorable instrument" and that what he did write "he stole from Locke's *Essays*." After the Federalists faded away and a new party system emerged, both parties claimed to be carrying on Jefferson's legacy, and both embraced the Declaration. Jefferson happily accepted the Declaration's new role. In 1824, when Congress sent him copies of a new facsimile edition, he expressed his pleasure at the evident "reverence for that instrument," which he viewed as "a pledge of adhesion to its principles and of a sacred determination to maintain and perpetuate them."

To later generations of Americans, the most important principle pledged in the Declaration was that of equality. Neither the Constitution nor the Bill of Rights asserted that all men were created equal. So it made sense that Americans seeking equality, whether workers or women or blacks, would turn to the Declaration. At the Seneca Falls Convention of 1848, women declared it "self-evident" that "all men and women are created equal." Abolitionists like William Lloyd Garrison urged, in 1847, the formation of a new government faithful to "the principles of the Declaration of Independence." At a Fourth of July celebration in 1852, Frederick Douglass asked the crowd: "Would you have me argue that man is entitled to liberty? That he is the rightful owner of his own body? You have already declared it." Most famously, in his 1863 Gettysburg Address, Abraham Lincoln looked back four score and seven years ago to 1776, the year "our fathers brought forth on this continent a new nation, conceived in liberty, and dedicated to the proposition that all men are created equal."

"a wall of separation between church and state"

What would liberty mean to people of different religions?

Mason's Declaration of Rights guaranteed freedom of conscience but still left the Anglican Church in a privileged position. Dissenters objected to this even before the Revolution, and they continued to pressure the General Assembly, arguing, for example, that they should not have to pay parish taxes and that their clergy ought to be able to perform legal marriages. In 1777, Jefferson drafted a "Bill for establishing religious freedom."

He explained his position memorably in his 1784 *Notes on the State of Virginia*. "The legitimate powers of government extend to such acts as are injurious to others," he wrote. "But it does me no injury for my neighbor to say there are twenty gods, or no god. It neither picks my pocket nor breaks my leg."

As it turned out, it took a lot longer for the delegates in Virginia to pass Jefferson's bill for religious freedom than it did for those in Philadelphia to adopt his Declaration. It was introduced to the House of Delegates in 1779 and tabled. It was not until 1785, by which time Jefferson was serving as ambassador to France, that an alliance of dissenters and rationalists, now led by Madison, pushed the act through the General Assembly. The Virginia Statute for Religious Freedom, as the bill became known once it became law, went into effect in 1786.

"Whereas Almighty God hath created the mind free," the Statute opened, "all attempts to influence it by temporal punishment or burdens, or by civil incapacitations . . . are a departure from the plan of the holy author of our religion." The Statute then decreed a separation of church and state: "No man shall be compelled to frequent or support any religious worship, place, or ministry whatsoever," and "all men shall be free to profess, and by argument to maintain, their opinion in matters of religion."

When Jefferson ran for president, his opponents branded him an atheist and infidel. This he was not: witness his invocation of an "Almighty God" in the opening line of the Statute. But Jefferson's religious beliefs certainly were not those of the Anglican establishment in which he was raised. He authored, for example, *The Life and Morals of Jesus of Nazareth*, begun in 1802 and finished in 1816. Here Jefferson compiled those parts of the New Testament he considered valid (the moral teachings of Jesus) and eliminated much of the rest (including references to the divinity of Jesus). The work was a private exercise that Jefferson never intended for publication, but it was nonetheless revealing.

While historians continue to debate Jefferson's private beliefs, none can question his conviction that religion was none of the government's business. In 1802, he explained that, unlike his predecessors in the presidency, he would not declare any days of thanksgiving and prayer, since religion was "solely between man and his God." Referring to the First Amendment of the Constitution, an amendment surely influenced by the Virginia Statute for Religious Freedom, Jefferson added: "I contemplate with sovereign reverence that act of the whole American people which declared that their legislature should 'make no law respecting an establishment of religion, or prohibiting the free exercise thereof,' thus building a wall of separation between church and state."

Jefferson's "wall of separation" has, perhaps, become a more familiar phrase than the actual language of the First Amendment. Various Supreme Court decisions have cited his words. In the 1947 case of *Everson v. Board of Education*, a New Jersey citizen objected to his town reimbursing parents for money they spent busing their children to Catholic parochial schools. Jefferson's wall, proclaimed Supreme Court Justice Hugo Black, "must be kept high and impregnable. We could not approve the slightest breach." There have nonetheless been many breaches, as Americans continue to debate such issues as whether prayers should be allowed in a school or whether the Ten Commandments can be displayed at a courthouse. Even the *Everson* decision, despite Black's sweeping statement, upheld the town's program on the grounds that it was designed to protect the students' safety.

Jefferson's commitment to the separation of church and state was literally set in stone. In 1826, when he reviewed his achievements and suggested what should go on his tombstone, Jefferson decided it ought to include his authorship of only two works: the Declaration of Independence and the Virginia Statute for Religious Freedom.

"I like a little rebellion now and then"

What really alarmed Jefferson's opponents were not his comments on religion but on rebellion. For Jefferson, the end of the Revolution did not signal the end of rebellion.

In 1787, Daniel Shays led several hundred men, incensed by high taxes and debts, in an attack on the federal arsenal in Springfield, Massachusetts. The attackers were repulsed, but many took it as a warning about the weakness of the federal government. The Articles of Confederation, adopted in 1777, made Congress almost entirely dependent on the states for money and troops. Many, not just in Massachusetts, resolved to fix the problem at the Constitutional Convention later in 1777.

For Jefferson, there was no problem to fix. "I hope they pardoned them," he wrote Abigail Adams in February about Shays and his followers. "The spirit of resistance to government is so valuable on certain occasions, that I wish it were to be always kept alive."

"I like a little rebellion now and then," he added. "It is like a storm in the atmosphere."

A few months later he expressed similar sentiments to Adams's son-in-law, William Stephens Smith. "What signify a few lives lost in a century or two?" he asked. "The tree of liberty must be refreshed from time to time with the blood of patriots and tyrants."

In 1789, when Paris was the scene of a far bigger rebellion than Shays's, Jefferson was there. The violence of the French Revolution did not change Jefferson's mind about the value of rebellion. In September, he philosophized, in a letter to Madison, about whether any generation has a right to bind another. "I set out on this ground, which I suppose to be self evident," he wrote, using language that could not but conjure up that of the Declaration, "that the earth belongs . . . to the living." Every law, even every constitution, would expire with the generation that created them. Jefferson even went so far as to define a generation as nineteen years.

Such comments were not just radical but downright anarchist. They seemed to confirm his opponents' worst fears. In reality, of course, Jefferson was not an anarchist. In 1787 he supported the Constitution, albeit with some reservations, and when he became president in 1801, he certainly did not dismantle the federal government. He did not demand that a new constitution and an entirely new set of laws be created every nineteen years. Still, these words do provide a window into Jefferson's thinking. Philosophically if not practically, he was deeply libertarian; he did not like government of any sort, and he wished for a world where none would exist.

"a government without newspapers or newspapers without a government"

Jefferson's libertarian principles did not always mesh with political realities. In principle, Jefferson believed in a strong press.

"Were it left for me to decide whether we should have a government without newspapers or newspapers without a government, I should not hesitate a moment to prefer the latter," he wrote Edward Carrington in 1787. Or this, to William Green Munford in 1799: "To preserve the freedom of the human mind . . . and freedom of the press, every spirit should be ready to devote itself to martyrdom."

Yet Jefferson also came to see himself as the victim of an abusive press. The press of the period was highly partisan and did not hesitate to attack the private lives of public figures. The Federalist press went after Jefferson with a vengeance. "It is well known," the *Richmond Recorder* wrote in 1802, "that the man, whom it delighteth the people to honor, keeps, and for many years past has kept, as his concubine, one of his own slaves. Her name is SALLY. . . . The name of her eldest son is TOM. His features are said to bear a striking, if sable resemblance to those of the president himself."

The charge that Jefferson had a slave mistress was picked up by other papers across the country. A Philadelphia magazine even set it to verse, to be sung to the tune of "Yankee Doodle":

Of all the damsels on the green
On mountain or in valley
A lass so luscious ne'er was seen
As Monticellan Sally.

By 1803, Jefferson was expressing some doubts about a completely free press. He suggested to Thomas McKean of Philadelphia that Republican governors sue Federalist editors for libel, explaining that "a few prosecutions of the most prominent offenders would have a wholesome effect in restoring the integrity of the presses."

Jefferson never abandoned his support for a free press. He never proposed anything along the lines of the Sedition Act the Federalists imposed in 1798, which prohibited inciting opposition to any act of Congress or the president. But his ringing endorsements of a free press came to be replaced by more cynical comments. In 1819 he wrote Nathaniel Macon that he read only one paper, the *Richmond Enquirer*, "and in that chiefly the advertisements, for they contain the only truths to be relied on in a newspaper."

"We have the wolf by the ears"

It was slavery, of course, that most clearly and most painfully highlighted the gap between Jefferson's principles and reality. In 1998, scientists found that Y-chromosome markers of Jefferson's descendants perfectly matched those of Sally Hemings's last son, Eston. Although this could mean one of Jefferson's male relatives was Eston's father, most historians concluded that the charges in the 1802 *Richmond Recorder* were true: Jefferson had a longstanding sexual relationship with a slave. And regardless of the nature of their relationship, no one could deny that Jefferson held Hemings and two hundred others as slaves.

Jefferson certainly understood the evils of slavery. "The whole commerce between master and slave is a perpetual exercise of the most boisterous passions, the unremitting despotism on the one part, and degrading submissions on the other," he wrote in *Notes*. "Our children see this, and learn to imitate it. . . . The parent storms, the child looks on, catches the lineaments of wrath, puts on the same airs in the circle of smaller slaves, gives a loose to his worst passions, and thus nursed, educated, and daily exercised in tyranny, cannot but be stamped by it with odious peculiarities." In 1770, he represented a mulatto man who had come to the general court in Williamsburg seeking freedom. Jefferson argued, albeit unsuccessfully, that "under the law of nature, all men are born free." In 1774, Jefferson prepared instructions he hoped the Virginia Convention would adopt for Virginia's delegates to a continental congress. Later published as *A Summary View of the Rights of British America*, it blamed King George III for vetoing colonial efforts to prohibit the slave trade. The Virginia Convention tabled Jefferson's proposal. And Jefferson's 1776 draft of a constitution for Virginia called for the gradual abolition of slavery.

After the 1787 publication of *Notes*, however, he was stunningly silent, perhaps because he had come to believe that free blacks and whites could never live together peacefully. *Notes*, which included both antislavery and clearly racist sentiments, spelled out Jefferson's reasons for pessimism: "Deep rooted prejudices entertained by the whites; ten thousand recollections, by the blacks, of the injuries they have sustained; new provocations; the real distinctions that nature has made; and many other circumstances, will divide us into parties, and produce convulsions which will probably never end but in the extermination of one or the other race."

On one of the few occasions later in his life that he did speak out on the subject, Jefferson threw his considerable weight behind slavery's expansion. The question of whether slavery should be allowed in Missouri woke Jefferson, he wrote to John Holmes of Massachusetts in 1820, "like a fire-bell in the night."

"There is not a man on earth who would sacrifice more than I would to relieve us from this heavy reproach [of slavery]," Jefferson continued, "in any practicable way. The cession of that kind of property . . . would not cost me a second thought, if, in that way, a general emancipation and expatriation could be effected."

The emphasis on expatriation, by which Jefferson meant sending slaves to Africa, underlined Jefferson's fear that free blacks could not live in peace with whites. "As it is," he told Holmes, "we have the wolf by the ears, and we can neither hold him, nor safely let him go. Justice is in one scale, and self-preservation in the other."

Jefferson chose self-preservation.

"Is it the Fourth?"

Despite his failure to live up to his own ideals, Jefferson retained the ability to inspire others to live by the principles he set forth in 1776. In 1826, as the fiftieth anniversary of the Fourth of July approached, officials in Washington invited him to attend. He was too ill, but he managed to send a written statement.

"The general spread of the light of science has already laid open to every view the palpable truth, that the mass of mankind has not been born with saddles on their backs, nor a favored few, booted and spurred, ready to ride them legitimately, by the grace of God," he wrote. "These are grounds of hope for others; for ourselves, let the annual return of this day forever refresh our recollections of these rights, and an undiminished devotion to them."

By the beginning of July, Jefferson realized he was dying. He faded in and out of consciousness.

"I remained at Monticello," his doctor Robley Dunglison later wrote, "and one of the last remarks he made was to me." About seven o'clock in the evening of July 3rd, Jefferson briefly awoke. In a voice Dunglison described as "husky and indistinct," Jefferson asked: "Is it the Fourth?" He died at about one o'clock the next day—July 4th.

CHAPTER 12

JOHN PAUL
JONES

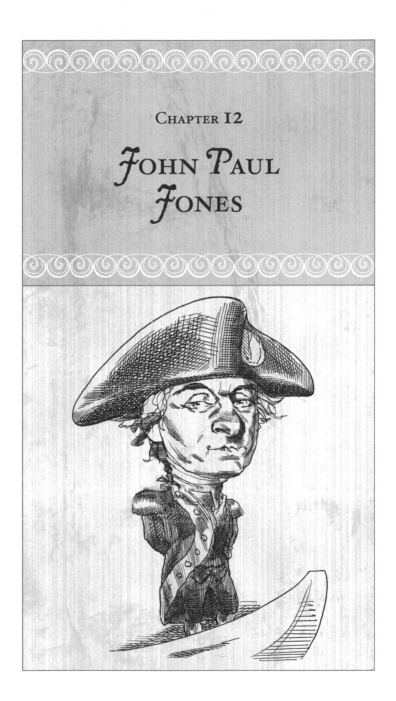

"I have not yet begun to fight"

I N THE HALLS of the British Admiralty, the American navy seemed unlikely to generate fear, or even notice. Of the fifty-seven ships the Americans used in the course of the Revolution—most of them merchant ships hastily and inadequately fitted for military service—thirty-four were sunk by the British or destroyed by the Americans to avoid capture. Even after the French joined the Americans, Britain ruled the seas.

Against this naval Goliath, the Americans sent a David by the name of John Paul Jones.

He was born John Paul, the son of the head gardener on a Scottish estate. At thirteen, he signed on as an apprentice on a ship. By 1773, he had worked his way up to captain of a merchant ship. Facing a mutiny, he killed one of the ringleaders, and fearing he might be charged with murder, he fled to Virginia—adding a new last name to make sure he couldn't be tracked down.

In 1775, John Paul Jones was commissioned in the Continental navy. Jones understood he couldn't match British firepower, that his only chance to make an impact was through hit-and-run raids on merchant ships and British coastal towns. "I wish to have no connection with any ship that does not sail fast," he wrote in the hope the French would provide him with what he needed, "for I intend to go in harm's way."

As captain of the *Ranger* in 1778, Jones managed a victory over HMS *Drake* and the theft, from the Earl of Selkirk's castle, of the family's silver. "The Pirate Jones," as he was known in England, was doing what he set out to do: the British, even the Admiralty, were nervous.

The battle—and the words—that made Jones famous came the next year. In 1779, Benjamin Franklin, then in Paris, helped Jones secure an old French merchant ship named the *Duc de Duras*. Jones renamed the ship *Bonhomme Richard*, after the "Poor Richard" of Franklin's popular *Poor Richard's Almanack*.

Jones left France in command of a squadron that included, besides the *Bonhomme Richard*, three smaller ships: the *Alliance*, the *Pallas*, and the *Vengeance*. It quickly became clear that the captains of the other three ships, especially Captain Pierre Landais of the *Alliance*, were privateers more interested in bounty than battles. As the ships circumnavigated the British Isles, Landais periodically disappeared.

On September 22nd, near Flamborough Head along England's Yorkshire coast, Jones spotted a convoy of more than forty British merchant ships accompanied by two warships, HMS *Serapis* and HMS *Countess of Scarborough*. Despite Jones' requests for a fast ship, his converted merchant ship was old and slow, but he had four armed ships to the British navy's two, and the *Bonhomme Richard* had a larger crew than the *Serapis*. Jones ordered his squadron to form a line of battle. The other captains, characteristically, ignored the order. Still, Jones sailed the *Bonhomme Richard* toward the *Serapis*. The *Serapis* fired a series a devastating broadsides at the *Bonhomme Richard*.

Jones's ship was a battered hulk. In his official report of the battle, Jones understated the desperate situation: "I must confess that the enemy's ship being much more manageable than the *Bonhomme Richard* gained thereby several times an advantageous situation in spite of my best endeavors to prevent it."

The battle certainly appeared lost to gunner's mate Henry Gardner. Not seeing Jones, assuming he was dead, and realizing the *Bonhomme Richard* was soon likely to sink or blow up, Gardner called "Quarters!"—a signal to the British that he was ready to surrender. Jones, furious, flung his gun at Gardner's head, knocking him out.

On the *Serapis*, Captain Richard Pearson had heard Gardner's calls and responded, "Have you struck? Do you call for Quarters?"

It was then, according to the *Bonhomme Richard*'s first lieutenant, Richard Dale, that Jones uttered his memorable line: "I have not yet begun to fight!"

The tide of battle turned when the *Serapis*'s bowsprit became entangled in the *Bonhomme Richard*'s starboard quarter. Realizing he could negate his opponent's superior speed and agility, Jones ordered grappling irons thrown over to hold the ships together. Pearson tried to break his ship away but couldn't. Bloody hand-to-hand fighting followed, and Jones's crew managed to blow up the gunpowder aboard the *Serapis*. The *Pallas* finally joined the fight, subduing the *Countess of Scarborough*. Even the *Alliance* got in the action, firing at the *Serapis*—though, given the proximity of the American and British ships, the shots ended up doing more damage to the *Bonhomme Richard* than to the *Serapis*.

About three hours after the battle began, with more than 150 of the Americans and more than 130 of the British dead or injured—about half of the crew members on both sides—Pearson surrendered. The *Bonhomme Richard* sank the next day, and Jones sailed on to Holland in the damaged but still seaworthy *Serapis*.

Jones's famous words have been the subject of much debate, with historians differing over at what point in the battle he spoke them and whether he spoke them at all. Only one person who was present at the battle quoted

Jones saying "I have not yet begun to fight." That was Dale, whose account did not appear until 1825, after John Henry Sherburne interviewed the former lieutenant for a biography of Jones.

Jones himself wrote two accounts of the battle. In his official report to Franklin, written October 3, 1779, he wrote that he answered Pearson "in the most determined negative." In an account he prepared for the French king, Louis XVI, he wrote that he said, "Je ne songe point a me rendre, mais je suis determine a vous faire demander quartier." Alas, we have only the French, which translates literally to "I haven't as yet thought of surrendering, but I am determined to make you ask for quarter."

Various accounts of Jones's words appeared in British newspapers at the time, not surprising given that more than a thousand people witnessed the battle from Flamborough Head, and that some British sailors escaped to shore in a rowboat. One account quoted Jones saying, "I may sink, but I'll be damned if I strike." Another had him answering Pearson, "No sir, I have not yet thought of it, but am determined to make you strike."

Whatever the exact words, there is no denying Jones loudly refused to surrender, then went on to win the battle. There is also no denying the effect of his victory. By taking the war to the shores of Great Britain, by defeating a British warship, Jones shattered the aura of invincibility surrounding the Royal Navy. Wrote the Earl of Carlisle: "Jones flings us all into consternation and terror, and will hinder Lady Carlisle's sea bathing." Less flippantly, the London *Daily Press* worried: "Instead of having the domain of the sea, it is now evident that we are not able to defend our coast from depredations." The British navy was of course still far superior to America's, and the Admiralty's decision to keep more ships at home was the result of its fear of a

French invasion, not Jones. Still, Jones's victory gave heart to Americans and support to those British who wondered whether subduing the colonies was worth the cost. Franklin rightly praised Jones for spreading "terror and bustle" along the British coasts.

Others followed Franklin's lead. A pirate to the British, Jones was a hero to generations of Americans. "We have not struck, he composedly cries, we have just begun," wrote Walt Whitman in *Song of Myself*. "The Coriolanus of the Sea," wrote Herman Melville in *Israel Potter*, a novel based on Jones's life. Jones also appeared as a character, sometimes fictionalized, in the works of James Fenimore Cooper, Alexandre Dumas, Rudyard Kipling, and William Thackeray. Theodore Roosevelt insisted, "Every officer should know by heart the deeds of John Paul Jones." Franklin Roosevelt wrote a screenplay based on Jones's life. Robert Stack played him in a 1958 movie.

Such posthumous praise was no consolation to Jones, who always longed to command a true squadron. Explaining to Thomas Jefferson that America "has no public employment for my military talents," Jones joined the Russian navy of Catherine the Great. Catherine was hardly the ideal leader for one who, in 1777, wrote Robert Morris that he fought "in defense of the violated rights of mankind." Indeed, Catherine was a far greater tyrant than George III ever was. But she had a fleet, and she was willing to give Jones command. In 1788, four years before his death in France, Jones led the Russian fleet to a series of victories over the Turks.

Chapter 13

Francis Scott Key

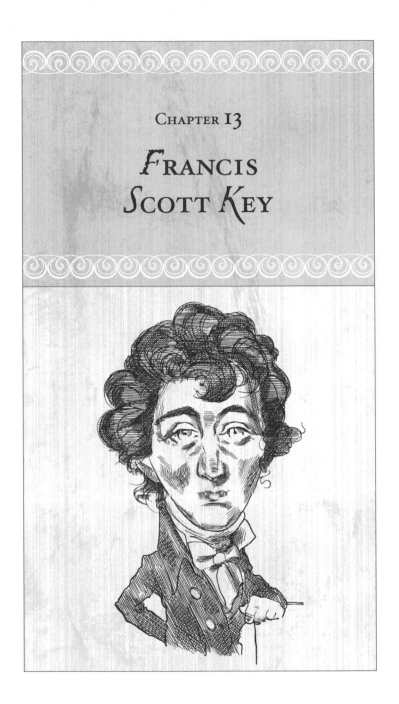

"O! say can you see"

A T THE Smithsonian Institution, you can see the flag that may have inspired the "The Star-Spangled Banner." It's huge—about a quarter of the size of a basketball court. Major George Armistead, commander of American forces at Baltimore's Fort McHenry, ordered it in 1813, because he wanted "a flag so large that the British will have no difficulty in seeing it from a distance." So this may very well have been the flag that the lawyer and sometime poet Francis Scott Key spotted "by the dawn's early light," indicating the Americans had withstood the British bombardment of the fort. But it was raining during the attack, and the fort may instead have used its smaller "storm flag," in which case that flag—since lost—may have been what Key saw on the morning of September 14, 1814. Whichever flag Key saw, it had "broad stripes and bright stars"—fifteen of each, to be precise. (It wasn't until 1818 that Congress set the number of stripes at thirteen and decided to add only stars for each new state.) And whatever flag Key saw that morning, he was so relieved to see it that he immediately scribbled the words that would become the national anthem.

By 1814, the War of 1812 was not going well for the Americans. An American expedition to Canada had failed, and with Napoleon defeated in Europe, the British could devote more resources to the war in America. In August the British easily captured Washington, D.C., burning the Capitol, Treasury, War Department, and the not-yet-painted-white President's House. They then prepared to attack Baltimore.

At this point Key emerged on the scene. He and John Skinner, the U.S. commissary general for prisoners, approached the flagship of the British force, the *Tonnant*, under a flag of truce. Their mission was to secure the release of Dr. William Beanes, a civilian who had been seized by the British. On September 7th, Key met with the British commander, General Robert Ross, aboard the *Tonnant*. Ross agreed to free Beanes but feared Beanes, Key, and Skinner might take back to Fort McHenry information about the British plans. He told all three they could not leave until after the battle.

The bombardment of Fort McHenry began on the morning of September 13th. "We were like pigeons tied by the legs to be shot at," recalled Judge Joseph H. Nicholson, who was second in command at the fort. Unlike Washington, however, Baltimore was well defended. At dawn, American private Isaac Munroe saw the flag rise above the fort. "Our morning gun was fired," Munroe wrote, "the flag hoisted, Yankee Doodle played, and we all appeared in full view of a formidable and mortified enemy, who calculated upon our surrender in 20 minutes after the commencement of the action." Key, aboard the truce ship tethered to the *Tonnant* about eight miles from the fort, also saw the American flag. Some have speculated that Beanes, who was nearsighted, might have asked the question that opened the poem: "O say can you see?" There's no evidence for this. The closest we have to an eyewitness report from the truce ship is that of Roger B. Taney. Taney, who later became chief justice of the Supreme Court, was Key's brother-in-law. In 1856, he wrote a letter in which he described a conversation he'd had with Key several weeks after the battle.

According to Taney, Key told him that until dawn he had no idea whether the fort had fallen. "They paced the deck for the residue of the night in painful suspense, watching with intense anxiety for the return of day, and looking every few minutes at their watches, to see how long they must wait for it;" wrote Taney, "and as soon as it dawned, and before it was light enough to see objects at a distance, their glasses were turned to the fort, uncertain whether they should see there the Stars and Stripes or the flag of the enemy. At length the light came, and they saw that 'our flag was still there.'"

Continued Taney: "He then told me that, under the excitement of the time, he had written a song and handed me a printed copy of 'The Star-Spangled Banner.' . . . He said he commenced it on the deck of the vessel, in the fervor of the moment, when he saw the enemy hastily retreating to their ships, and looked at the flag he had watched for so anxiously as the morning opened." According to Taney, Key began writing the poem "upon the back of a letter which he happened to have in his pocket," and finished it as the boat made its way back to Baltimore.

Nicholson, who besides being second in command at the fort was also Key's brother-in-law, greatly admired the poem and arranged for it to be printed in handbill form. This circulated around Baltimore with the title "The Defence of Fort McHenry" and with a note that it went with a tune for "Anacreon in Heaven." This was a song written for a British gentlemen's club around 1775 and well-known in both England and America. At some point, Key gave the song its current name, and its popularity gradually spread, especially during the Civil War and the Spanish-American War. By 1900, both the army and navy played it more often than either "Yankee Doodle" or "Hail Columbia." Soon it became a pregame ritual at baseball games, and eventually some fans would quip that its final words were not "O'er the Land of the Free, and the Home of the Brave," but rather "Play Ball!"

In 1931, Congress considered whether to declare Key's poem the national anthem. "The Star-Spangled Banner" had its detractors. The *New York Herald Tribune*, for example, commented that it had "words that nobody can remember to a tune that nobody can sing." Prohibition was still in effect, and some objected to an anthem whose tune was thought (wrongly) to be an old drinking song. Others objected to its militarism, especially in the third stanza, which describes the British forces as "the hireling and slave." (Though few know the words to more than the first stanza, the anthem actually has four.) Nonetheless, Congress declared it America's anthem.

"In God is our Trust"

In the final stanza of Key's poem, the penultimate couplet reads: "Then conquer we must, when our cause it is just, / And this be our motto— 'In God is our Trust.'" This final stanza has led some to credit Key not only with the national anthem but also with the national motto—"In God We Trust"—still found on American coins and bills.

The connection between Key's words and the national motto is, alas, tenuous. It was not until 1861, forty-seven years after the composition of "The Star-Spangled Banner," that Secretary of the Treasury Salmon P. Chase wrote Director of the Mint James Pollock that "the trust of our people in God should be declared on our national coins." Pollock proposed three possibilities: "Our Country" or "Our God" or "God Our Trust." In 1863, Chase suggested instead "In God We Trust." A year later, Congress approved minting coins with Chase's words. In 1956, in the midst of the Cold War against the atheist Soviet Union, Congress officially declared "In God We Trust" the national motto.

Like the national anthem, the national motto has had plenty of critics, including those who have argued that it violates the First Amendment prohibition of any law respecting "an establishment of religion." The motto has so far withstood all court challenges, most notably that of *Aronow v. United States*. In 1970, the 9th U.S. Circuit Court of Appeals ruled that the motto was "of patriotic or ceremonial character and bears no true resemblance to a governmental sponsorship of a religious exercise."

Might Key's words have inspired Chase? It's possible, but there's no evidence to support the claim, and Key was certainly neither the first nor the last to suggest that Americans ought to trust in God.

CHAPTER 14

JAMES
MADISON

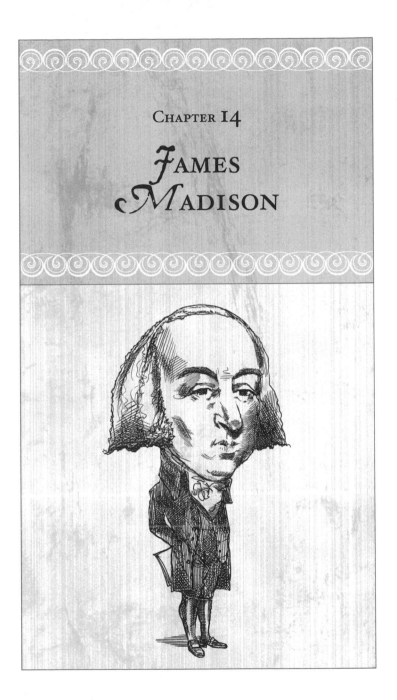

"If men were angels, no government would be necessary"

THOUGH HE was called, even in his own lifetime, the "Father of the Constitution," James Madison never attained the public stature of his good friend Thomas Jefferson. Part of the problem was that he never attained Jefferson's physical stature: Jefferson was about six-foot-two or three, Madison no more than five-six. It also didn't help that Madison's best-remembered act as president was fleeing Washington, along with his wife, Dolley, when the British burned the capital during the War of 1812. Nor could Madison claim to have written the Constitution in the sense that Jefferson wrote the Declaration. "This was not like the fabled goddess of wisdom the offspring of a single brain," he explained in 1834. "It ought to be regarded as the work of many heads and many hands."

Nonetheless, it is hard to imagine the Constitution without Madison's head and hand. He was the most creative political theorist of the founders, and at the Constitutional Convention of 1787 he transformed theory into a workable government. The first government of the United States, which was based on the Articles of Confederation signed during the Revolution, was most definitely not working. The Confederation was less a national government than an alliance of independent states. Congress had no power to tax, and its resolutions were little more than recommendations. The states clashed over funding, over boundaries, over trade regulations, over how to deal with local rebellions. William Grayson, a member of Congress from Virginia, expressed the frustration of many in 1786 when he described the weakness of the federal government: "If it remains much longer in its present state of imbecility," he said, "we shall be one of the most contemptible nations on the face of the Earth."

The Constitutional Convention that convened the next year in Philadelphia had as its stated aim the revision of the Articles, but the terms of the debate quickly changed when, on May 29, 1787, Governor Edmund Randolph presented what became known as the Virginia Plan. This was no revision; it was an entirely new plan of government. It was also, despite contributions from George Mason, George Wythe, and George Washington, largely Madison's plan.

The Virginia Plan proposed replacing the Continental Congress with a three-part government consisting of legislative, executive, and judicial branches. The legislative branch would consist of two houses, with the number of representatives from each state determined either by the state's population or the amount it paid in taxes. To secure the Convention's support, Madison reluctantly agreed that all states would have two senators, rather than the proportional representation Madison advocated—and that still applied for the House of Representatives. Still, the Constitution that came out of Philadelphia was very much Madison's concept.

Another key compromise, designed to satisfy southerners, was that representation in the House would be based on the number of free persons plus three-fifths of "all other persons," meaning slaves. Like Jefferson, Madison disliked slavery and wished it would go away; also like Jefferson, he did little to make that wish come true. In this sense, too, the Constitution was very much Madison's.

Next, nine of the thirteen states had to ratify the Constitution. Anti-Federalists such as Patrick Henry and George Mason vehemently protested the proposed government's powerful central government, its usurpation of states' rights, its susceptibility to the control of a moneyed aristocracy. In essays printed in newspapers throughout America, anti-Federalists argued that the Constitution would create a government as tyrannical as the one against which they had fought the Revolution. One argument that the Federalists, who supported the Constitution, found particularly difficult was that a large republic would inevitably be destroyed by the existence of so many different factions, each pursuing its own self-interest rather than the common good.

Federalists responded with a propaganda campaign of their own, and again Madison played a crucial role. Along with Alexander Hamilton and John Jay, he wrote a series of eighty-five essays in support of ratification. They were first published in the New York *Independent Journal* and later published as *The Federalist*. Here Madison turned on its head the standard wisdom that only a small and homogenous democracy like that of ancient Athens could survive. "Passion never fails to wrest the scepter from reason," he wrote in *Federalist* 55. "Had every Athenian citizen been a Socrates, every Athenian assembly would still have been a mob."

Better then, he argued, to build a government that accepted that people would pursue their own interests and that would make use of the very passions usually thought to be the Achilles heel of democracy. "Ambition must be made to counteract ambition," he wrote in *Federalist* 51. "If men were angels, no government would be necessary. If angels were to govern men, neither external nor internal controls on government would be necessary."

Just as each of the three branches of government would provide checks and balances on the others, a "multiplicity of interests" would protect rather than destroy the people's liberties. "The influence of factious leaders may kindle a flame within their particular States, but will be unable to spread a general conflagration through other States," Madison wrote in *Federalist* 10. "A rage for [any] improper or wicked project . . . will be less apt to pervade the whole body of the Union than a particular member of it."

"Congress shall make no law"

What anti-Federalists objected to most was the Constitution's lack of a bill of rights. Back in 1776, many states—notably Virginia—had adopted, in addition to constitutions, declarations guaranteeing such rights as freedom of the press and religion. Richard Henry Lee, a leading anti-Federalist, bemoaned the lack of any words in the Constitution protecting "those essential rights of mankind without which liberty cannot exist."

The Federalist response was that a bill of rights at the federal level wasn't necessary. The Constitution did not grant the federal government any power over the press or religion, for example. "Can the general government exercise any power not delegated to it?" Madison asked the Virginia convention called to consider the Constitution. "If an enumeration be made of our rights, will it not be implied, that every thing omitted, is given to the general government?" The real danger to liberty, Madison believed, came not from government officials but from the people themselves who, if a cause was sufficiently popular, would readily trample over a minority's rights. In such cases a mere "parchment barrier" like a bill of rights would do no good.

Or so Madison argued at both the Constitutional Convention and the Virginia ratifying convention. And yet, once the Constitution was ratified and Madison was elected to the nation's first Congress, he became the most adamant and persistent proponent of a bill of rights. Indeed, he was as much the father of the Bill of Rights as he was of the Constitution.

What caused such a dramatic turnaround?

To a large extent, it was political expediency. Better to adopt an unnecessary but basically harmless bill of rights than to let the anti-Federalists call a new convention that might come up with something as ineffectual as the Articles of Confederation. A bill of rights might also help ensure the anti-Federalists' loyalties to the new government. So Madison, campaigning for a seat in the first Congress, provided one of the nation's earliest examples of what later would be known as a flip-flop.

Anti-Federalists continued to distrust Madison. They enlisted James Monroe, a Revolutionary War hero (who at more than six feet towered over Madison), to run against him. Madison was forced to hit the campaign trail, which was especially cold and snowy in the winter of 1788–1789. Again and again, he pledged he would work for a bill of rights. In a January 1789 letter, written to a Baptist minister named George Eve and intended for wider distribution, Madison conceded he had originally opposed the idea "as calculated . . . to furnish the secret enemies of the Union with an opportunity of promoting its dissolution." But "circumstances are now changed," he continued, and with the Constitution ratified, "amendments, if pursued with a proper moderation and in a proper mode, will be not only safe, but may serve the double purpose of satisfying the minds of well meaning opponents, and of providing additional guards in favour of liberty."

Madison would, he assured Eve, support "provisions for all essential rights." The pledge paid off; Madison received 1,308 votes to Monroe's 972.

True to his word, on June 8, 1789, Madison introduced in Congress his amendments to the Constitution. Drawing heavily on the Virginia Declaration of Rights, he insisted on, among other rights, freedom of religion, speech, press, and assembly; the right to bear arms; and various guarantees of a fair trial. If Madison expected others in Congress to rally behind him, he was quickly disappointed. Federalists continued to put forward the same objections Madison himself had once put forward: a bill of rights was unnecessary, premature, and counterproductive. Besides, with the Constitution now ratified, many Federalists no longer felt any need to mollify their opponents. Anti-Federalist congressmen, for their part, preferred a much more radical rewrite of the Constitution, one that would restore the primacy of individual states. And many congressmen, both Federalists and anti, thought they ought to let the government run for awhile so they could better identify its flaws before trying to correct them.

Still, Madison persisted, so much so that he must have been motivated by more than political expediency. True, in private he still described them as "the nauseous project of amendments." But the tenacity with which he pushed the amendments through a reluctant Congress could only have been motivated by a genuine belief in their value. "If all power is subject to abuse," he told Congress in June, "then it is possible the abuse of the powers of the [central] government may be guarded against in a more secure manner than is now done. . . . We have in this way something to gain, and, if we proceed with caution, nothing to lose." This was Madison the crusader for liberty, the same man, after all, who in 1776 had presented an amended version of

George Mason's Declaration of Rights in order to strengthen the provision protecting religious freedom, and who in 1785 had steered through Virginia's legislature Thomas Jefferson's Statute for Religious Freedom.

The amendments he presented to Congress on June 8th were not in the form we now recognize them. Rather than add them at the end of the Constitution, where Madison felt they might be ignored as some sort of footnote, he proposed placing them within the body of text, and he gave specific instructions as to how to edit the Constitution accordingly. Madison's work was revised first by a House of Representatives committee, which presented its version in late July. A month later the House as a whole passed its version, which moved the amendments to the end of the Constitution. Madison continued to lobby his colleagues until September, when the Senate passed its version and then Congress sent twelve amendments to the states.

The states rejected the first two amendments—the first of which would have regulated the size of the House of Representatives, the second of which (ultimately ratified in 1992) regulated how Congress could give itself raises. It was therefore entirely unintentional that the most famous words in the Bill of Rights were bumped up from the third to the first amendment: "Congress shall make no law," the amendment now read, "respecting an establishment of religion, or prohibiting the free exercise thereof; or abridging the freedom of speech, or of the press, or the right of the people peaceably to assemble, and to petition the Government for a redress of grievances."

By the end of 1791, ten states had ratified the ten amendments, officially making them part of the Constitution. In March 1792, Secretary of State Thomas Jefferson informed the states of their approval: "I have the honor to send you herein enclosed," he wrote, "two copies duly

authenticated of an act concerning certain fisheries of the
United States, and for the regulation and government of
the fishermen employed therein; also of an act to establish
the post office and post roads within the United States; also
the ratifications by three fourths of the legislatures of the
several states, of certain articles in addition and amendment of the Constitution of the United States."

Thus was the nation informed—after a notice about
fishing and the post office—of the Bill of Rights, words
that have become, perhaps second only to the Declaration
of Independence, America's most sacred text. Madison's
worry about the placement of the Bill of Rights was certainly misplaced. Far from leading to its being forgotten or
ignored, separating the Bill of Rights from the main text
of the Constitution has allowed future generations to focus
on them. Perhaps, too, it has allowed us to recognize the
shortcomings of the original Constitution and to treat it
not as a finished work but as a living document, a continuing experiment in democracy.

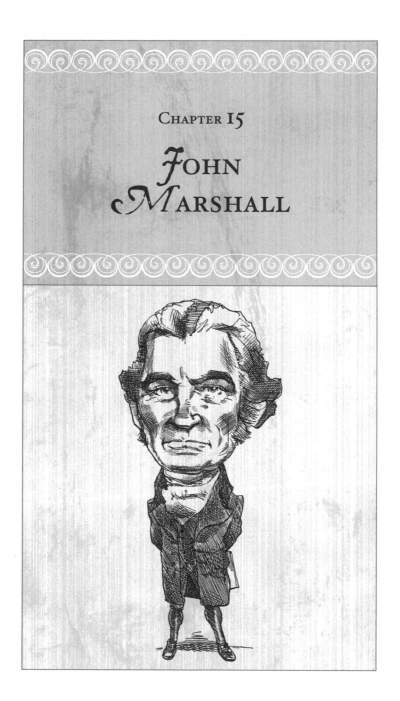

Chapter 15

John
Marshall

"An act of the legislature, repugnant to the Constitution, is void"

HAVING LOST the 1800 election to Thomas Jefferson, President John Adams looked for ways to preserve some of his administration's legacy. On March 2, 1801, two days before his term expired, Adams appointed forty-two judges for the nation's capital. All were members of Adams's lame duck Federalist Party. The president signed the commissions, then forwarded them to his secretary of state, John Marshall. Marshall had himself just been appointed to a new job—a considerably more important end-of-term Adams appointment as the new chief justice of the Supreme Court. Perhaps with that on his mind, Marshall affixed the presidential seal to the justice-of-the-peace commissions and then forgot about them. He left them on a table in the State Department, and there Jefferson found them when he took office. Jefferson was understandably annoyed by Adams's effort to ram these Federalist "midnight judges" down the throats of a Republican administration. He accepted twenty-five of Adams's forty-two but instructed his new secretary of state, James Madison, to ignore the rest of the commissions, including that of William Marbury, a prominent local businessman. Marbury appealed to the courts, and in 1803, the Supreme Court—now with Marshall presiding—ruled in the case of *Marbury v. Madison*.

As chief justice, Marshall faced a predicament. He knew Marbury's commission had the presidential seal—

Marshall had affixed it himself. Yet if the court ordered Madison to appoint Marbury, Madison might very well ignore the ruling, and the Supreme Court would be revealed as powerless. Rather than directly confront the power of the presidency, Marshall instead took on Congress, ruling that the Judiciary Act of 1789, which authorized the Court to issue a writ compelling Madison to deliver the commission, was unconstitutional. It was a brilliant political move: Marbury would not get his appointment, so Jefferson and Madison could not object. At the same time, Marshall had bestowed upon the Supreme Court the power of "judicial review." With this power to declare acts of Congress unconstitutional, the Supreme Court, which Alexander Hamilton had in 1788 described as "beyond comparison the weakest of the three branches" of government, now emerged as equal to the executive and legislative branches.

Lest anyone fail to notice, Marshall's opinion spelled out its significance. "An act of the legislature, repugnant to the Constitution, is void," Marshall proclaimed. "This theory is essentially attached to a written constitution, and is consequently to be considered, by this Court, as one of the fundamental principles of our society."

Who was responsible for determining what acts were repugnant to the Constitution? Marshall left no doubt about that: "It is emphatically the province and duty of the judicial department to say what the law is."

Marshall did not invent the concept of judicial review, which had roots in colonial and state experiences as well as constitutional theory. Still, *Marbury v. Madison* was the first time the Supreme Court had declared an act of Congress unconstitutional. The Court, from then on, held the power to interpret the Constitution.

"The government of the Union is, emphatically and truly, a government of the people"

Marshall wielded that power—and further expanded the power of the Court—in a series of landmark decisions, most notably in the 1819 case of *McCulloch v. Maryland*. Here the Court upheld the constitutionality of the Bank of the United States. William McCulloch, a cashier at the Baltimore branch of the bank, had been sued by the state of Maryland for issuing notes without paying a state tax. Marshall saw this as a contest between state and federal power, and he came down decisively on the side of the latter.

"The government of the Union," he declared in words not so different from those of Abraham Lincoln's later Gettysburg Address, "is, emphatically and truly, a government of the people. In form and in substance it emanates from them. Its powers are granted by them, and are to be exercised directly on them, and for their benefit."

Maryland's attempt to tax the Bank of the United States was an attack not just on the federal government but on the American people. "The power to tax involved the power to destroy," Marshall exclaimed in another oft quoted line. If states could tax the bank, "they may tax the mail; they may tax the mint; they may tax patent rights; they may tax the papers of the custom house; they may tax judicial process; they may tax all the means employed by the government." This, Marshall concluded, "was not intended by the American people. They did not design to make their government dependent on the states." *McCulloch v. Maryland* was a ringing endorsement of federal supremacy, a stinging rejection of the doctrine of "states' rights."

"The people made the Constitution, and the people can unmake it"

Two years after *McCulloch v. Maryland*, in *Cohens v. Virginia*, Marshall again sided with the federal government against a state. Philip and Mendes Cohen managed a company that sold national lottery tickets in Norfolk, Virginia. The sales were authorized by Congress to raise money for the District of Columbia. Virginia, which had its own lottery, outlawed the sale of out-of-state lottery tickets and fined the Cohens $100. The Cohens appealed to the Supreme Court. Marshall determined that Congress had not intended to authorize the sale of lottery tickets in Virginia; on the merits of the case, therefore, he upheld the Cohen's conviction. More importantly, though it did the Cohens no good, Marshall again reiterated the right of the federal government—and the Court—to determine these matters.

"The people made the Constitution, and the people can unmake it," Marshall wrote. "But this supreme and irresistible power to make or to unmake resides only in the whole body of the people, not in any subdivision of them." The "whole body" was the federal government, the "subdivision"—clearly subordinate—any state.

Not surprisingly, such words did not sit well with proponents of states' rights, including Jefferson. Jefferson, who was Marshall's second cousin, had disliked Marshall since childhood. His animosity only grew as Marshall became one of the most powerful exponents of a powerful federal government that Jefferson feared threatened the liberties for which Americans had fought the Revolution. Jefferson advised Supreme Court Justice Joseph Story to be wary of Marshall's deceptive powers of persuasion.

"You must never give him an affirmative answer or you will be forced to grant his conclusion," Jefferson said. "Why, if he were to ask me if it were daylight or not, I'd reply, 'Sir, I don't know, I can't tell.'"

Marshall, too, had little good to say about his cousin. "What you say of Mr. Jefferson," he told Story, "rather grieves than surprises me. It grieves me because his influence is still so great that many . . . will adopt his opinions however unsound they may be." Marshall added that Jefferson "is among the most ambitious, and I suspect among the most unforgiving of men" and that "he looks . . . with ill will at an independent judiciary."

It was, of course, Marshall's vision of a powerful national government and a powerful Supreme Court that ultimately became reality, and Marshall has deservedly received much credit for that. "If American law were to be represented by a single figure," wrote Supreme Court Justice Oliver Wendell Holmes in 1901, "skeptic and worshipper alike would agree without dispute that the figure could be one alone, and that one, John Marshall."

Marshall died in 1835. His funeral procession wound through the streets of Philadelphia, coincidentally on the anniversary of the date in 1776 when the Liberty Bell celebrated American independence. While tolling for John Marshall, the bell cracked. It never rang again.

CHAPTER 16

GEORGE MASON

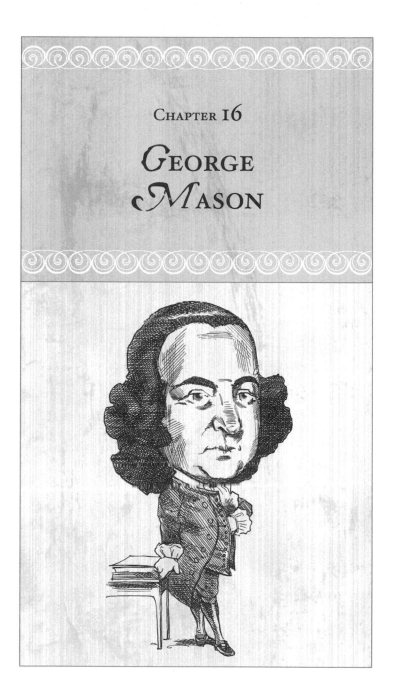

"All men are by nature equally free and independent . . ."

A ND HAVE certain inherent rights . . . namely, the enjoyment of life and liberty . . . and pursuing and obtaining happiness."

Sound familiar?

It's not the Declaration of Independence. But Thomas Jefferson certainly drew on these words from Virginia's Declaration of Rights when he declared that "all men are created equal," that they have "certain unalienable rights," and that "among these are life, liberty and the pursuit of happiness." The 1776 Virginia Declaration also served as a model, in 1789, for the Bill of Rights of the United States Constitution and for the Declaration of the Rights of Man and the Citizen, which was to the French Revolution what Jefferson's was to the American.

The Declaration of Rights came out of the fifth Virginia Convention, which convened in Williamsburg in May 1776. This was not quite a year after George III declared the colonies to be in a state of rebellion. Nearby Norfolk lay in ruins, and though it was unclear whether British or Continental soldiers were to blame, there was no question that Virginia was at war. The delegates had their hands full coping with everything from a Norfolk petition asking how to choose its delegates since the courthouse there had burned, to one from a soldier asking for aid since his "right arm was unfortunately taken off by a cannon ball." The fighting became fully and formally a revolution on May 15th. On that day, the Convention passed without opposition a resolution instructing its delegates in Philadelphia to introduce a resolution in the Continental Congress proposing independence. On June 7th, Virginia's Richard Henry Lee carried out those instructions. "These United Colonies," the resolution read, "are, and of right ought to be, free and independent states."

The May 15th vote in Williamsburg also served as Virginia's own declaration of independence. Immediately, the British flag was taken down from the capitol's cupola, replaced by the flag of George Washington's army.

Having severed ties with Great Britain, the Convention's next order of business was to create a new government for Virginia. It was an indication of just how important the delegates considered a citizen's inherent rights that, before getting down to work on a constitution, they first set out to write a declaration of rights. The purpose, wrote Edmund Randolph, then a delegate and later the author of a history of Virginia, was so that "in all the revolutions of time, of human opinion, and of government, a perpetual standard should be created, around which the people might rally and by a notorious record be forever admonished to be watchful, firm and virtuous."

The Convention appointed a committee of thirty-six members. This was at best an inefficient approach, especially since, as Randolph put it, many of the members had an "ardor for political notice rather than a ripeness in political wisdom." Then arrived George Mason, a delegate from Fairfax County who was, as his biographer Robert A. Rutland put it, a "reluctant statesman." Mason considered public service "an unjust and oppressive invasion of my personal liberty," and he must have greeted his election to the Convention (by a narrow margin) with mixed feelings. He delayed leaving his home in Virginia's Northern Neck (not far from Mount Vernon) because of what he called a "smart fit of the gout." The remedies of the time—which ranged from ginseng to bloodletting—surely did not improve his mood, nor did the bumpy five-day carriage ride.

Mason was nonetheless held in high esteem by his contemporaries, and as soon as he reached Williamsburg, he was added to the committee. He surveyed the situation with characteristic disdain. "The committee appointed to prepare a plan is, according to custom, over-charged with useless members," Mason wrote to Richard Henry Lee, who as a Virginia delegate to the Continental Congress put forth the resolution for independence. "We shall, in all probability have a thousand ridiculous and impracticable proposals."

The only hope, Mason concluded, was to put "this business" in the hands of "a few men of integrity and abilities, whose country's interest lies next their hearts" He clearly had himself in mind. Mason established himself in a room at the Raleigh Tavern and got to work on a draft.

Now there was reason for optimism. Edmund Pendleton, the Convention's president, wrote Jefferson, who along with Lee was representing Virginia in Philadelphia: "the political cooks are busy in preparing the dish, and as Colo. Mason seems to have the ascendancy in the great work, I have sanguine hopes it will be framed so as to answer its end, prosperity to the community and security to individuals." Randolph later confirmed that Mason's work "swallowed up all the rest."

Mason's draft opened with the words that Jefferson would later rephrase: "That all men are born equally free and independent, and have certain inherent natural Rights, of which they can not by any compact, deprive or divest their posterity; among which are the enjoyment of life and liberty, with the means of acquiring and possessing property, and pursuing and obtaining happiness and safety." The draft then declared principles of government, among them that its power derived from the people, that a majority had the right to change a government, that hereditary privileges had no place in this government, that there should be a separation of powers and frequent elections, that a person accused of a crime had the right to a trial by jury and the right not to incriminate himself, and that there should be religious toleration.

The committee made various changes to Mason's draft, including prohibiting cruel and unusual punishment, guaranteeing freedom of the press, subordinating military to civilian power, and broadening the definition of religious toleration to guarantee that "all men are equally entitled to the free exercise of religion according to the dictates of conscience."

Even these changes, however, were to some extent Mason's work.

On May 27th, the committee sent its report to the full Convention, and on June 1st it was printed in the *Virginia Gazette*. At this point the delegates were preoccupied by the movement of British forces and they thereby required adjustments to Virginia's defensive positions. Nonetheless, Robert Carter Nicholas, the delegate from James City County, quickly homed in on the problem that bedeviled the founders again and again: How could they reconcile the declaration that all men were "equally free" with the practice of slavery? How could you guarantee every man's right to property, when that property included other men? It was Pendleton, this time, who found the way around the seemingly absolute language. Pendleton suggested adding a phrase clarifying that the freedom applied only to men "when they enter into a state of society." Since the delegates all understood blacks could not enter into Virginia society, slaveholders could endorse the Declaration. On June 12th, the Virginia Convention adopted the document. (As it turned out, the final version of the Declaration of Rights was largely ignored; it was the committee's draft that, after appearing in the *Gazette*, was picked up by other newspapers and went on to influence the Declaration of Independence, the Bill of Rights, and the Declaration of the Rights of Man and the Citizen.)

Next, Mason moved on to writing Virginia's constitution. Here he had some serious competition. Jefferson, still in Philadelphia, was working on his own version and felt sufficiently strongly about it that he asked to be recalled to Williamsburg. After all, he wrote, the design of a new government "is the whole object of the present controversy; for should a bad government be instituted . . . it [would have] been as well to have accepted at first the bad one offered to us from beyond the water without the risk and expence of contest." By the time Jefferson's version reached Williamsburg, however, the Convention had already pretty much settled on Mason's. The delegates added a few clauses from Jefferson's, but, as George Wythe explained to his friend in Philadelphia, Jefferson could not expect further revisions on "a subject the members seemed tired of." On June 29th, the Convention adopted the constitution. The delegates then put it into effect by electing Patrick Henry governor.

Mason was pleased with both the Declaration and constitution. "We have laid our new government on a broad foundation, and have endeavoured to provide the most effectual securities for the essential rights of human nature," he wrote. "I trust that neither the power of Great Britain, nor the power of hell will be able to prevail against it."

Mason, of course, did not invent the principles in the Declaration. He drew on British documents, including the Magna Carta of 1215, the Petition of Rights of 1628, the Habeas Corpus Act of 1679, the Bill of Rights of 1689, and the Act of Settlement of 1701. Colonial charters and practice also influenced his work, as did the writings of political philosophers such as John Locke. Still, it was Mason who merged the British and colonial traditions into a single document that became a model for other states and nations.

Why, then, is Mason so little known today? One reason is that he never wrote his memoirs or made any effort to preserve his papers. A bigger reason is that, unlike such fellow Virginians as Washington, Jefferson, and Madison, Mason never sought higher office. When chosen as a senator, he declined. Indeed, his major foray into national politics was as an anti-Federalist, politicking against adoption of the United States Constitution. Among his objections to the Constitution was the absence of a declaration of rights like that he wrote in 1776.

Mason was hardly the only prominent anti-Federalist; in Virginia, Patrick Henry also adamantly opposed the Constitution. Still, Mason's testiness alienated his fellow founders and perhaps historians as well. Mason's neighbor George Washington said that "to alarm the people seems to be the groundwork of his plan" and came to refer to Mason as his former friend. Other Federalists alluded to Mason's "madness" or "the effects of his age" on his mind. ("Sir," the always blunt Mason supposedly replied to one such critic, "when yours fails nobody will ever discover it.")

Mason must have felt at least somewhat vindicated when, in 1791, a year before his death, Virginia became the tenth state to ratify the first ten amendments to the United States Constitution, thereby giving America its Bill of Rights. And, though Mason remains a largely forgotten founder, Jefferson understood what he owed him. In his *Autobiography*, he described Mason as "a man of the first order of wisdom among those who acted on the theatre of the revolution, of expansive mind, profound judgment, cogent in argument, learned in the ore of our former constitution, and earnest for the republican change on democratic principles."

CHAPTER 17

JAMES OTIS

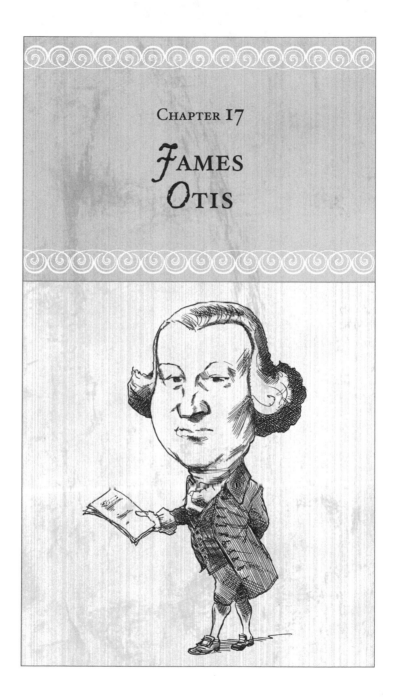

"Taxation without representation is tyranny"

THE WORDS that became a rallying cry for eighteenth-century revolutionaries—and for anti-tax movements throughout American history—are generally attributed to James Otis, a man John Adams called "a flame of fire."

Otis's skills as an orator became clear in a Boston courtroom in 1761. Otis, a lawyer representing local merchants, transformed a technical and legal dispute involving British customs practices into one of the earliest and most dramatic statements of colonial opposition to parliamentary regulation. Adams, who was in the courtroom, vividly recalled the scene. "With the promptitude of classical allusions, a depth of research, a rapid summary of historical events and dates, a profusion of legal authorities, a prophetic glare of his eyes into futurity, and a rapid torrent of impetuous eloquence, he hurried away every thing before him. American independence was then and there born," Adams wrote in 1817 to William Tudor, who later wrote a biography of Otis. "Then and there was the first scene of the first act of opposition to the arbitrary claims of Great Britain. Then and there the child Independence was born. In fifteen years, namely in 1776, he grew up to manhood, and declared himself free."

A year later, in another letter to Tudor, Adams quoted Otis's most famous words. "Since the [1761] debate," wrote Adams, "and since it was known that the acts of trade were to be enforced, and a revenue collected by authority of Parliament, Mr. Otis's maxim, that 'taxation without representation was tyranny,' and that 'expenditures of public money, without appropriations by the representatives of the people, were unconstitutional, arbitrary, and therefore tyrannical,' had become popular proverbs."

There are reasons to doubt whether Otis deserves quite as much credit as Adams gave him. For one thing, as Tudor asserted in his 1823 biography, Otis may have been quoting Josiah Child, a seventeenth-century London merchant and economist who advocated a liberal trade policy. Moreover, Adams was writing more than fifty years after Otis would have uttered the phrase, and he was writing with an agenda of his own: he wanted Tudor to write a work that would restore what Adams saw as the rightful place of Massachusetts patriots (including Otis and Adams) at the forefront of the Revolution. This place, Adams felt, was threatened by William Wirt's recently published biography of the Virginian, Patrick Henry. "In the month of February, 1761," Adams wrote Wirt, also in 1818, "James Otis electrified the town of Boston, the province of Massachusetts Bay, and the whole continent, more than Patrick Henry ever did in the whole course of his life. . . . If Mr. Henry was Demosthenes . . . James Otis was Isaiah and Ezekiel united."

Whatever Adams's bias, he was adamant, as he told Tudor, that Otis's words became "commonplace observations in the streets." And there's no denying that Otis spoke strongly about the injustice of taxation without representation in the widely read pamphlet of 1764, "The Rights of the British Colonies Asserted and Proved." "I can see no reason to doubt but that the imposition of taxes . . . in the colonies is absolutely irreconcilable with the rights of the colonists as British subjects and men," Otis wrote in "Rights." "The very act of taxing exercised over those who are not represented appears to me to be depriving them of one of their most essential rights as freemen." So, even if historians don't fully trust Adams and can't be certain about whether Otis actually spoke his most famous words, Adams may have been right about Otis's influence.

Ironically, it was ultimately not Virginia's patriots but those in Massachusetts who cast Otis aside. At no point, for all his protests about taxation and representation, did Otis question the fundamental right of a British Parliament to govern America. "The power of Parliament is uncontrollable but by themselves, and we must obey," he wrote in "Rights." "There would be an end of all government if one of a number of subjects or subordinate provinces should take upon them so far to judge of the justice of an act of Parliament as to refuse obedience to it."

What, then, could the colonists do if an act—or a tax—was unjust? Well, Otis argued, all they had to do was point out the problem and Parliament would surely fix it. "Parliaments repeal such acts as soon as they find they have been mistaken," he explained in "Rights." "See here the grandeur of the British constitution! See the wisdom of our ancestors! . . . To preserve [this constitution] has cost oceans of blood and treasure in every age; and the blood and the treasure have upon the whole been well spent." Otis's 1765 pamphlet "A Vindication of the British Colonies" offered comparable praise: "The British constitution of government as now established in his Majesty's person and family, is the wisest and best in the world . . . and his subjects the happiest in the universe."

Such faith in the British constitution was common in the 1760s, and Otis could point to the repeal of the Stamp Act as an example of parliamentary reconsideration and reason. Ten years later, though, it was no longer possible for revolutionary leaders to assume that Parliament would always act reasonably, let alone in the interest of the colonies. Otis's arguments were seen as craven submission or, at best, confused; Otis himself as irrelevant or, worse, a Tory. By 1776, "A Friend to Liberty" could ask in the *Boston Evening-Post*: "How can such inconsistencies and prevarications be reconciled to honesty, patriotism and common sense?" Adams recalled that Otis was called "a reprobate, an apostate, and a traitor, in every street in Boston."

He was also called a madman, and during the 1770s he did indeed suffer lengthy bouts of mental instability.

What caused Otis to go insane remains a subject of debate. Clifford Shipton, whose portrait of Otis in *Sibley's Harvard Graduates* was highly unflattering, stated that "From his youth Jemmy showed the queerness which was to develop into the insanity of his later years." Biographer John J. Waters blamed a combination of Otis's family history, the ambiguity of his politics, and the growing popularity of other Massachusetts politicians like Samuel Adams. Historian Gordon Wood suggested Otis's "frantic attempts" to reconcile conflicting philosophies "formed the crisis of his life and helped to tear his mind to pieces."

Others blamed a brawl with a British customs official. Otis, though too moderate to satisfy more radical Bostonians, was nonetheless associated with them in the minds of many loyal to the Crown, and he was very upset to hear British customs officials had called him a traitor to his country. In September 1769 Otis ran into one of these officials, John Robinson, at a Boston coffee house. Robinson tried to twist Otis's nose, leading to an exchange of blows in which each attacked the other with fists and canes. Otis left bleeding from a gash in his head. He appeared to recover and successfully sued Robinson for damages, but according to historian Samuel Eliot Morison, "the crack on his head permanently unhinged his reason."

Adams, while insisting on the importance of Otis's early words, recognized that his later political positions and his mental health presented problems. "He talks so much and takes up so much of our time and fills it with trash, obsceneness, profaneness, nonsense and distraction," wrote Adams in a 1770 diary entry. "In short, I never saw such an object of admiration, reverence, contempt, and compassion, all at once." In 1783, the man whom Adams described as "a flame of fire" was struck by lightning and died.

"No taxation without representation"

The origins of "No taxation without representation"—a phrase very similar to Otis's and more familiar to modern ears—are even murkier. Some modern sources attribute it to Jonathan Mayhew, but they include no eighteenth-century reference. The phrase has not been found in Mayhew's writings. Nor, as in Otis's case, has it been found in Adams's writings. So it's by no means clear that Mayhew deserves the credit for these particular words.

But Mayhew, a Boston preacher, did rail against "arbitrary taxes," usually from the pulpit of Boston's West Church and often to the dismay of his more conservative parishioners. And Adams, in an 1818 letter to the newspaper publisher Hezekiah Niles, did lavish praise on Mayhew for having "spread a universal alarm against the authority of Parliament." Again countering Wirt's claim that it was Henry who gave "the first impulse to the ball of independence," Adams provided his ranking of the "most conspicuous" Massachusetts leaders: Otis was first, with Mayhew coming right after Samuel Adams and John Hancock.

These were the men, Adams told Niles, who "produced, in 1760 and 1761, an awakening and a revival of American principles and feelings, with an enthusiasm which went on increasing till, in 1775, it burst out in open violence, hostility, and fury."

CHAPTER 18

THOMAS PAINE

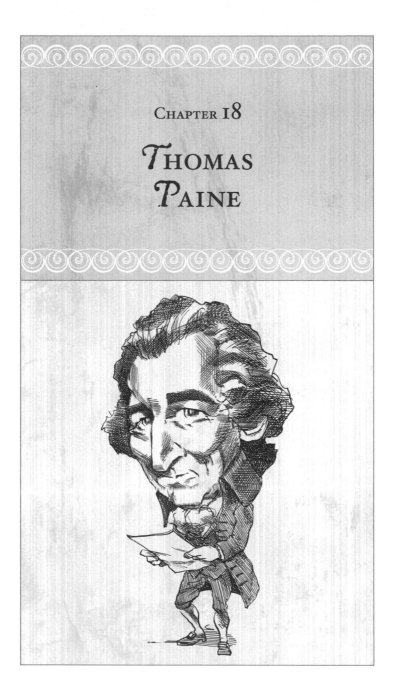

"We have it in our power to begin
the world over again"

EVEN AFTER shots had been fired at Lexington and Concord, even as the Continental Congress berated King George III and Parliament, as the year 1776 began, most Americans did not think they were fighting for independence. They were, they insisted, merely demanding their rights as freeborn Britons.

The Bostonian James Otis, who had declared back in 1764 that Americans could not be "taxed without their own consent," argued that this was so because "every British subject born on the continent of America [is] entitled to all the natural, essential and inseparable rights of our fellow subjects in Great Britain." Tellingly, he added: "We love, esteem, and reverence our mother country, and adore our King." Thomas Jefferson, writing in late 1775, maintained "there is not in the British Empire a man who more cordially loves a union with Great Britain than I do."

All that changed in January 1776, when an anonymous forty-six-page pamphlet called "Common Sense" appeared in Philadelphia. The author was soon revealed to be Thomas Paine, a working-class immigrant who had arrived from England in 1774 with a letter of introduction from none other than Benjamin Franklin, whom Paine had met in London. Franklin recommended Paine as "an ingenious worthy young man."

Ingenious indeed. Paine's words recast the Revolution as about something more—much more—than British policies or taxes. It was not even about Great Britain or America.

"The cause of America is in a great measure the cause of all mankind," Paine proclaimed. "We have it in our power to begin the world over again. The birthday of a new world is at hand."

No longer, after reading Paine, were Americans demanding their rights as British subjects. What they now sought were their rights as American citizens. Paine's cause—and America's—was now freedom.

The impact of "Common Sense" was quick and huge. Within a few months hundreds of thousands had read the pamphlet—the equivalent of more than twenty million today.

It was not just Paine's ideas that so excited people but also the way he expressed them. Unlike most political writers of the time, Paine was not writing for an educated elite. "As it is my design to make those that can scarcely read understand," he later wrote, "I shall therefore avoid every literary ornament and put it in language as plain as the alphabet." John Adams, who some at first thought the pamphlet's author, readily conceded that he "could not have written any thing in so manly and striking a style." Thomas Jefferson agreed: "No writer has exceeded Paine in ease and familiarity of style, in perspicuity of expression, happiness of elucidation, and in simple and unassuming language." Jefferson's Declaration of Independence listed the injuries done to the colonies by George III, but only Paine referred to the king as the "royal brute" and the "crowned ruffian."

"There is something very absurd in supposing a continent to be perpetually governed by an island," Paine insisted. "For God's sake, let us come to a final separation."

These were passionate words, and passions were inflamed. "We were blind, but on reading these enlightening words the scales have fallen from our eyes," a Connecticut reader wrote to the *Pennsylvania Evening Post* in February 1776.

George Washington, who himself gave up on reconciliation with Britain after reading "Common Sense," told his secretary that the pamphlet was "working a powerful change." New Yorker Hugh Hughes told Samuel Adams that "it is certain there never was anything printed here within these thirty years or since . . . that has been more universally approved or admired." Virginian Edmund Randolph later recalled "the ease with which it insinuated itself into the hearts of the people." Franklin, happy to take credit for his role in Paine's success, frequently mentioned the pamphlet's "great effect on the mind of the people."

Granted, "Common Sense" benefited in part from timing. A year earlier, let alone a decade, Americans might not have been ready to hear such a radical message, or at least to embrace it publicly. But there's no question that Paine's writings expressed the case for independence in a way that moved Americans to action.

"These are the times that try men's souls"

Winning that independence was another matter. By November 1776, Washington and his troops, having fled across New Jersey, were holed up on the Pennsylvania side of the Delaware River. Paine was among those men.

By the light of a campfire, Paine again wrote words that would change the course of American history.

"These are the times that try men's souls," went the first of Paine's "American Crisis" essays. "The summer soldier and the sunshine patriot will, in this crisis, shrink from the service of his country; but he that stands it now, deserves the love and thanks of man and woman. Tyranny, like hell, is not easily conquered; yet we have this consolation with us, that the harder the conflict, the more glorious the triumph."

The pamphlet appeared in December and had the immediate effect of inspiring crucially needed new recruits to enlist. Then, on Christmas Eve, Washington ordered "American Crisis" read aloud to the troops. With Paine's words fresh in their minds, they set off across the icy Delaware River. Fighting a blizzard, frostbite, and exhaustion, they launched a successful attack on the Hessian mercenaries in Trenton.

After the American Revolution was won, Paine turned his attention to Europe. A story—perhaps apocryphal— has it that Benjamin Franklin once said, "Where liberty is, there is my country." To which Paine responded: "Where liberty is not, there is my country." In England in 1791, he wrote the first part of "Rights of Man," defending the French Revolution and calling for a revolution in England. "Rights of Man" was in some ways a "Common Sense" for the British, but it went further. This was a work that would have pleased a twenty-first-century social democrat. Wrote Paine in the second part of "Rights of Man," published in 1792: "When, in countries that are called civilized, we see age going to the workhouse and youth to the gallows, something must be wrong in the system of government."

"Rights of Man" sold hundreds of thousands of copies in Britain, a country where there were no more than four million literate people. It also led to a warrant for Paine's arrest on charges of treason. Paine fled to France, and in 1792 he was granted citizenship and a seat in the French National Convention.

For once, Paine was not radical enough. Though he was of course no monarchist, he argued that Louis XVI ought not to be executed. Maximilien-Francois-Marie-Isidore de

Robespierre, the Jacobin leader who dominated the revolutionary government during what became known as the Reign of Terror, called for action against foreign conspirators. On Christmas Eve of 1793, Paine was arrested.

In prison Paine continued to work on his latest work, "The Age of Reason," which appeared between 1794 and 1796. This time Paine took on the power of organized religion, writing that "all national institutions of churches, whether Jewish, Christian or Turkish, appear to me no other than human inventions, set up to terrify and enslave mankind, and monopolize power and profit."

Paine spent ten months in prison. He became increasingly furious at the American government, which he feared would end up, under Washington, as a monarchy. Paine's fury was personal as well as political: though James Monroe, as the American ambassador to France, eventually helped secure his release, Paine felt the American government, especially Washington, had not done enough to help him. "He can serve or desert a man, or a cause, with constitutional indifference," Paine wrote of Washington, "and it is this cold hermaphrodite faculty that imposed itself upon the world and was credited for a while, by enemies as by friends, for prudence, moderation and impartiality."

In 1802, at the invitation of Jefferson, Paine returned to America. His return was anything but triumphant. The Federalist press, always eager to portray the president as a radical, saw an opportunity to embarrass Jefferson. The *Gazette of the United States* reported that "the President of the United States had written a very affectionate letter to that living opprobrium of humanity, Tom Paine, the infamous scavenger of all the filth which could be raked from dirty paths which have been hitherto trodden by all the revilers of Christianity." Boston's *Mercury and New-England Palladium* called Paine a "lying, drunken, brutal infidel."

Paine was not an atheist. It was organized religion, not God, that "The Age of Reason" decried. Paine rejected the Bible but believed God had created the universe. This was a deism in some ways like that of Jefferson or Franklin. But Jefferson and Franklin, while questioning the divinity of Jesus, admired his teachings and attended church services. The vehemence of Paine's antireligious rhetoric stood out, and Christians would not forgive or forget it. Paine's attacks on Washington—himself almost a god—also didn't help. Paine's reputation never fully recovered.

John Adams, who conceded Paine's significance but feared his radicalism, vented his anger—and perhaps some envy—in 1805. "I am willing you should call this the Age of Frivolity, as you do; and would not object if you had named it the Age of Folly, Vice, Frenzy, Fury, Brutality, Demons, Buonoparte, Tom Paine, or the Age of the burning . . . pit; or anything but the age of Reason," he wrote Benjamin Waterhouse.

Continued Adams:

> I know not whether any man in the world has had more influence on its inhabitants or affairs for the last thirty years than Tom Paine. There can be no severer satire on the age. For such a mongrel between pigs and puppy, begotten by a wild boar on a bitch wolf, never before in any age of the world was suffered by the poltroonery of mankind to run through such a career of mischief. Call it then the Age of Paine.

When Paine died in 1809, six mourners attended his funeral. Even Jefferson eventually distanced himself. When asked for permission to print his correspondence with Paine, he refused. "No, my dear sir, not for all this world," he exclaimed. "Into what a hornet's nest it would thrust my head!" In the 1880s Theodore Roosevelt called Paine a "filthy little atheist," and in most histories Paine is given at most a secondary role in the Revolution.

Paine was never entirely forgotten. Abraham Lincoln said, "I never tire of reading Paine." Social critics ranging from William Lloyd Garrison and Susan B. Anthony to Emma Goldman and Eugene Debs continued to draw on his work. Three months after the attack on Pearl Harbor, Franklin Roosevelt referred to the times that try men's souls. Even Ronald Reagan quoted him, telling the 1980 Republican convention that it had the power to begin the world over again. Still, when people think of America's founding fathers, Paine's name is rarely among the first mentioned.

Even Paine's bones were lost to history. A decade after Paine's death, the British political writer William Cobbett, unhappy that Paine was not properly honored in America, dug up the remains from a New York cemetery and carried them to England. Exactly what happened to them after that is unclear. In his 1995 book, Paul Collins attempted to trace the fate of Paine's bones, and came up with theories that were plausible though not definitive.

"Where is Tom Paine?" Collins asked in his book's penultimate line. His answer: "Reader, where is he not?"

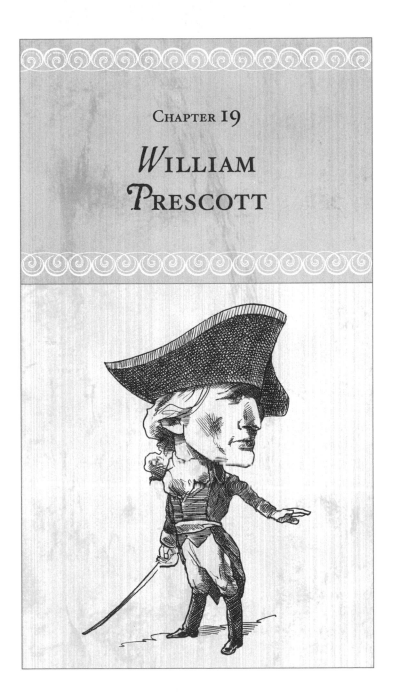

CHAPTER 19

WILLIAM PRESCOTT

"Don't fire till you see the whites of their eyes"

PARTICIPANTS could not agree what to call the Battle of Bunker Hill: it was actually fought on nearby Breed's Hill, and many referred to the battle as such. They also were unsure who won the battle: the British emerged with control of both hills, but General Thomas Gage, who commanded all British forces in North America, wrote soon after that "the loss we have sustained is greater than we can bear." So it's hardly surprising that also in dispute is who first uttered the famous words associated with the place.

On this much all agreed: unlike the skirmishes at Lexington and Concord, Bunker Hill was the first true battle of the Revolution. After chasing the British troops from Lexington and Concord back to Boston in April 1775, the Americans surrounded the city. Gage called the siege a "preposterous parade of military arrangement," and British General John Burgoyne referred to the Massachusetts troops as "rabble in arms." Still, Gage could not help but be concerned when, on the morning of June 17th, he awoke to find that about 1,600 Americans had, under cover of night, occupied nearby Charlestown peninsula and fortified Breed's Hill there. This put American cannons dangerously within range of British ships and troops.

One of the American generals on the peninsula was Israel Putnam, a hero of the French and Indian War who had survived capture by the Iroquois and a shipwreck off the coast of Cuba. The other was William Prescott, whom Gage spotted that morning through his telescope. Gage turned to Colonel Josiah Willard and asked if he knew the rebel commander. Willard told Gage it was his brother-in-law.

"Will he fight?" asked Gage, according to an 1847 account of the battle.

"Prescott will fight you to the gates of hell," Willard answered.

Gage knew he had to dislodge the Americans from the hill, and he ordered General William Howe to lead about 2,300 British troops up the hill. Twice, the Americans pushed them back. On their third try the British prevailed. It was during that final British attack, with the Americans running out of ammunition, that either Putnam or Prescott gave the famous order.

The earliest printed account of the words came in Mason Weems's 1808 biography of George Washington:

> The Americans are all wound up to the height of the enthusiasm of liberty, and . . . lying close behind their works, with fowling-pieces loaded with ball and buck-shot, wait impatiently for the approaching enemy. . . .
> "Don't throw away a single shot, my brave fellows," said old Putnam, "Don't throw away a single shot, but take good aim; nor touch a trigger, till you can see the whites of their eyes."

This being the same Weems who invented the story of George Washington and the cherry tree, there is reason for skepticism.

Unlike George's "I can't tell a lie," however, the words from Breed's Hill were later corroborated by eyewitnesses. In his 1818 *History of Bunker Hill Battle*, Samuel Swett described the scene as the British approached:

Putnam rode through the line, and ordered that no one should fire till they arrived within eight rods, nor any one till commanded. "Powder was scarce and must not be wasted. They should not fire at the enemy till they saw the whites of their eyes, and then fire low, take aim at their waist-bands. They were all marksmen, and could kill a squirrel at a hundred yards; reserve their fire, and the enemy were all destroyed. Aim at the handsome coats, pick off the commanders." The same orders were reiterated by Prescott at the redoubt, by Pomeroy, Stark, and all the veteran officers.

In the appendix to his book, Swett quoted three soldiers—John Stevens, Elijah Jourdan, and Philip Johnson— who recalled that it was Putnam who first gave the order, "Don't fire till you see the whites of their eyes."

Still, there were also many eyewitnesses who recalled that Prescott, not Putnam, was in command at Breed's Hill, and that Prescott must therefore have first spoken the words. The case for Prescott was further buttressed by the general's own letter to John Adams, written just two months after the battle. Though Prescott didn't quote himself saying the famous words, he did recall giving an order along the same lines:

> The enemy advanced and fired very hotly on the fort, and meeting with a warm reception, there was a very smart firing on both sides. After a considerable time, finding out ammunition was almost spent, I commanded a cessation till the enemy advanced within thirty yards, when we gave them such a hot fire that they were obliged to retire nearly one hundred and fifty yards before they could rally.

In Richard Frothingham's 1851 history of the siege and battle, the words were attributed to the "officers" rather than to one in particular. But by the late nineteenth century, most historians had concluded, like Justin Winsor in 1887, that "it seems well established that Col. William Prescott commanded at the redoubt, and no one questioned his right." More recent historians have generally agreed on the command and the quote; in 1975, for example, Henry Steele Commager and Richard B. Morris referred to "Prescott's immortal words."

Lost amid the battle between partisans of Putnam and Prescott was that whoever first spoke the words at Breed's Hill may have been quoting a Prussian officer who served under Frederick the Great decades before the American Revolution. In his 1881 history of the siege of Boston, Everett Hale wrote: "All along the American lines the order had been given which the officers remembered in the memoirs of Frederick's wars: 'Wait till you can see the whites of their eyes.'" In a footnote, Hale attributed the line to a Prince Charles fighting at Jagendorf in 1745. If so, proponents of Putnam or Prescott could at least take consolation in knowing that Charles was urging his troops to keep quiet so they could sneak up on the enemy, a very different reason for holding fire than the shortage of ammunition at Bunker Hill. Besides, some historians such as J. L. Bell have raised doubts about whether Charles actually said the line, and even if he did, whether Putnam or Prescott was familiar with it.

For Putnam and Prescott, the pressing issue was not who spoke the words associated with Bunker Hill but rather who won the battle there. The immediate result clearly favored the British, who took both Bunker Hill and Breed's Hill. But, as Gage conceded, the cost was huge. More than 226 British soldiers were dead and 828 wounded, compared to American losses of 140 and 271. Reeling from the casualties, Gage chose not to pursue the Americans, which gave them time to regroup. In July, George Washington took command of the main American army in Cambridge, Massachusetts, and the Americans gradually increased enlistments. In January, Colonel Henry Knox delivered to Washington forty-five captured British cannons he had hauled over snow and ice from Fort Ticonderoga on Lake Champlain. In March, the British abandoned Boston.

Of Bunker Hill, concluded Gage: "I wish this cursed place was burned."

CHAPTER 20

PAUL REVERE

"One, if by land, and two, if by sea"

L ISTEN, MY children, and you shall hear / Of the midnight ride of Paul Revere," wrote Henry Wadsworth Longfellow. Since Longfellow's poem was published in 1861, generations of children have listened, and generations of historians have catalogued the poet's errors.

Longfellow's Revere starts by telling a friend that, if British troops march from Boston, he should hang a lantern from the city's North Church tower as a signal: "One, if by land, and two, if by sea; / And I on the opposite shore will be." So debunkers have also tended to start with the lantern, noting that the silversmith-patriot, far from waiting for the signal on the "opposite shore," was in Boston arranging for a friend to send the signal. They have also proven beyond any doubt that Revere did not, as Longfellow had it, row himself alone across the Charles River. Nor was it Revere alone who spread "his cry of alarm" to "every Middlesex village and farm." Revere didn't even make it to Concord, where the recently roused patriots gathered to protect their munitions from the British. Other rowers and other riders, though largely forgotten, played key roles that night of April 18, 1775. In 1896, Helen More took it upon herself to tell the story of one of them:

> Tis all very well for the children to hear
> Of the midnight ride of Paul Revere;
> But why should my name be quite forgot
> Who rode as boldly and well, God wot?

Why, should I ask? The reason is clear—
My name was Dawes and his Revere.

More's task, of course was hopeless; Revere, not William Dawes, was permanently ensconced in the American imagination. But what of it? For Paul Revere fully deserved his place in history. He was not, to be sure, the solitary rider of Longfellow's poem, but he was one of the organizers of a sophisticated intelligence network in and around Boston. As Revere recalled in a 1798 letter to Jeremy Belknap of the Massachusetts Historical Society, he was, in the fall of 1774 and the spring of 1775, "one of upwards of thirty, chiefly mechanics, who formed our selves into a committee for the purpose of watching the movements of the British soldiers." When the British prepared to move, numerous sources let Revere know that "something serious" was up. They suspected the British would head toward Lexington in an effort to capture John Hancock and Samuel Adams, both of whom were staying at the parsonage of Reverend Jonas Clark there, or toward Concord, where the patriots had stored arms and ammunition.

Revere had already told patriot leaders in Charlestown what the signal would be: "I agreed with a Col. Conant, and some other gentlemen, that if the British went out by water, we would show two lanthorns in the North Church steeple; and if by land, one."

On the evening of April 18th, Revere "called upon a friend, and desired him to make the signals." Then Revere met the two other friends who rowed him across the Charles, slipping by a British warship. In Charlestown, Conant and others had seen the signal and had "a very good horse" ready for Revere. He was spotted by two British officers but escaped and "alarmed almost every house, till I got to Lexington."

"The British are coming"

About midnight, Revere arrived at the Clark parsonage. Here he found his way blocked not by the British but by Sergeant William Munroe of the Lexington militia. About fifty years later, Munroe recalled the events of the night. "I told him," said Munroe, "the family had just retired, and had requested, that they might not be disturbed by any noise about the house. 'Noise!' said he, 'you'll have noise enough before long. The regulars are coming out.'"

Munroe did not quote Revere as saying, "the British are coming." Nor did any other witness, including Revere in his 1798 letter to Belknap or in a 1775 account given to the Massachusetts Provincial Congress. Nor, it must be added, did Longfellow put in Revere's mouth any words about the British coming. Where that part of the legend originated is unclear. What is clear is that Revere, like other patriots, would have referred to the British troops as Regulars, or perhaps Redcoats. To have called them British would merely have confused those whom he was alarming, most of whom still thought of themselves as British. Though the first shots of the Revolution were soon to ring out, the Declaration of Independence was still more than a year away.

Whatever words it took, Revere awoke Hancock and Adams and then set off from Lexington to Concord. He was joined by Dawes, a Boston tanner who had taken a different route to Lexington, alerting villages and farms along his way. Revere and Dawes then met Samuel Prescott, a young Concord doctor who had been in Lexington courting his fiancée. Prescott offered to help, pointing out (Revere told Belknap) that since people in the area knew him, they "would give the more credit to what we said."

About halfway to Concord, the three ran into a patrol of six British officers. Dawes and Prescott escaped, the former taking refuge in an abandoned farmhouse and the latter continuing on to Concord to complete Revere's mission. Revere was captured and escorted back toward Lexington. As they neared the town, Revere told the British officers five hundred patriots would soon be gathered nearby. He was bluffing, but the officers decided that they ought to warn their commanders and that Revere would only slow them down. They released the prisoner.

Back in Lexington, at about 3 a.m. Revere returned to Clark's house. To his distress, he discovered Hancock and Adams were still there. He accompanied them toward Woburn, where the two patriot leaders would be safe, since the British didn't know they were there (though Hancock somewhat undermined these security measures by insisting on sending his carriage back to Lexington to pick up a fresh salmon he'd left there and now wanted to eat). Revere returned to Lexington yet again, and yet again was distressed by what he found. About seventy-five minutemen had gathered in town but, seeing no British soldiers, they had retired to a local tavern. Fortunately, another messenger soon arrived, informing them the British were approaching.

The first shots were fired around dawn. Badly outnumbered, the minutemen retreated, and the British moved on to Concord. There they faced a more substantial force of about seven hundred patriots, who forced the British back to Boston. Patriots harassed the British throughout the retreat, firing on them from behind houses, barns, trees, and walls.

From a strictly military perspective, the events of April 18th and 19th were not particularly important. Still, this was definitely a patriot victory and, as the first battle of the Revolution, of great psychological significance. Why, then, did American mythmakers not stick to the facts? In part,

Americans—as Longfellow realized—have always idolized loners. "From Captain John Smith to Colonel Charles Lindbergh," wrote historian David Hackett Fischer, "many American heroes have been remembered that way, as solitary actors against the world." Longfellow's Revere certainly fit the mold.

Long before Longfellow, though, Revere's story was already being molded to fit needs other than historical accuracy. Ironically, patriot lore at first ignored Revere entirely. The patriots' main concern was portraying themselves as innocent victims of British aggression, and the existence of Revere's elaborate alarm system, fully activated before any British attack, undercut the case. Patriot storytellers were especially eager to establish that the British fired first at Lexington, and Revere's 1775 account to the Massachusetts Provincial Congress was of no use. Revere did not take part in the fighting at Lexington and Concord (he was busy at the time hiding some papers that Hancock and Adams left behind and that the British would certainly have found both revealing and treasonable), so all he could say was that he heard a shot and saw some smoke.

Revere's subsequent military career was also a great disappointment, not least to Revere himself. In 1779, he commanded artillery in a disastrous attack against a British fort in Maine. When Brigadier General Peleg Wadsworth ordered Revere to give up his boat to evacuate the crew of another, Revere refused. At a court-martial three years later, Revere was acquitted, though his reputation was damaged by the testimony of Wadsworth, who said Revere refused to give up the boat because "he had all his private baggage at stake." Here is another irony, almost surely the greatest, of Revere's story: Peleg Wadsworth, the general who questioned Revere's patriotism, was the grandfather of Henry Wadsworth Longfellow.

CHAPTER 21

TACHNEDORUS

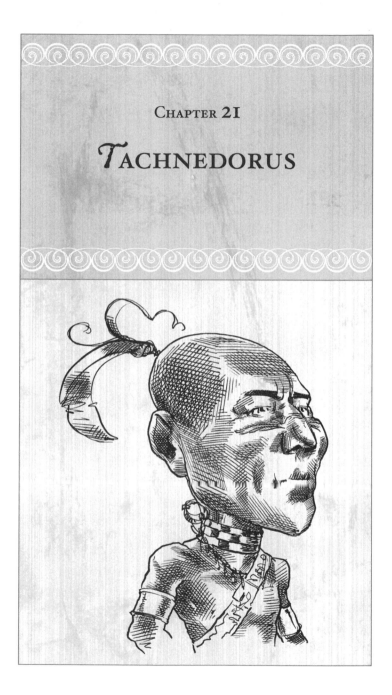

"Who is there to mourn for Logan? Not one"

IN HIS *Notes on the State of Virginia*, Thomas Jefferson refuted some common racist assumptions about Indians. "Of their bravery and address in war we have multiplied proofs," Jefferson declared, "because we have been the subjects on which they were exercised. Of their eminence in oratory we have fewer examples, because it is displayed chiefly in their own councils."

Yet there was at least one Indian orator, Jefferson continued, who was the equal of Demosthenes and Cicero. This was John Logan, a Mingo chief also known as Tachnedorus. In 1774, the troops of Lord Dunmore, the last royal governor of Virginia, overwhelmed Shawnee, Delaware, and Mingo warriors, and forced the Natives to surrender all their territory south of the Ohio River. Logan refused to sign the peace treaty, and he sent an explanation to Dunmore by messenger. These words, which Jefferson printed in his *Notes* as an example of Indian eloquence, came to be known as Logan's Lament:

> I appeal to any white man to say, if ever he entered Logan's cabin hungry, and he gave him not meat; if ever he came cold and naked, and he clothed him not. During the course of the last long and bloody war, Logan remained idle in his cabin, an advocate for peace. Such was my love for the whites, that my countrymen pointed as they passed, and said, "Logan is the friend of white men." I had even thought to have lived with you, but for the injuries of one man. Col. Cresap,

the last spring, in cold blood, and unprovoked, murdered all the relations of Logan, not sparing even my
women and children. There runs not a drop of my
blood in the veins of any living creature. This called on
me for revenge. I have sought it: I have killed many: I
have fully glutted my vengeance. For my country, I
rejoice at the beams of peace. But do not harbor a
thought that mine is the joy of fear. Logan never felt
fear. He will not turn on his heel to save his life. Who
is there to mourn for Logan? Not one.

James Madison was also impressed enough by the
Lament, which he called a "specimen of Indian eloquence
and mistaken valor," to want to see it published. In January 1775, he sent a version of the speech almost identical
to that in Jefferson's *Notes* to the *Pennsylvania Journal*,
which became the first newspaper to publish it. Two weeks
later, a less polished version appeared in the *Virginia
Gazette*.

Acclaimed by Madison and Jefferson, the Lament
struck a chord in the new nation. Throughout the nineteenth century and into the twentieth, it was reprinted
numerous times, including in Washington Irving's *Sketch-
Book* and the McGuffey Readers. It was memorized by
countless schoolchildren who must have appreciated, if not
its eloquence, at least its brevity. (The Lament has twenty
fewer words than the Gettysburg Address.)

The Lament also inspired a great deal of controversy.
In Jefferson's *Notes*, first published in 1785, he—like
Tachnedorus in the Lament—blamed Michael Cresap for
starting the war. It was Cresap, according to Jefferson, who
after two Shawnees murdered a white frontiersmen, led a
party intent on revenge. Even before killing the canoe full
of women and children who happened to be Logan's fam-

ily, Cresap had been "infamous for the many murders he had committed on those much-injured people."

In 1797, Maryland attorney general Luther Martin questioned Jefferson's version. Martin claimed that Cresap had not been present at the murder of Logan's family. Martin clearly had an axe to grind: not only was he a member of the anti-Jefferson Federalist Party but he was also Cresap's son-in-law. Still, Jefferson took the charge seriously. He gathered testimony from witnesses and in an appendix to the 1801 edition of the *Notes* revised his story somewhat. Jefferson now concluded that three sets of murders had set off Lord Dunmore's War, and that Cresap had perpetrated two of them but not the third.

There the matter stood until 1851 when Brantz Mayer, president of the Maryland Historical Society, revealed that Jefferson had suppressed key evidence. Specifically, Mayer found among Jefferson's papers a 1798 letter from General George Rogers Clark. Responding to Jefferson's call for testimony that he could include in his 1801 appendix, Clark wrote that Cresap was not present at the murder of Logan's family. Since Clark was with Cresap much of 1774, his testimony was certainly relevant. And since Clark and Jefferson were old friends, Jefferson must have considered him a credible witness. Yet amid the extensive correspondence published in the appendix Clark's letter is nowhere to be found.

Why did Jefferson suppress Clark's letter?

Some historians have concluded that Jefferson simply didn't want to undermine the case against Cresap. He may have been certain of Cresap's guilt, and there was plenty of other evidence against the frontiersman, which Jefferson presented in the appendix. Jefferson's defenders also noted that Brantz's book was hardly a model of objectivity. In his eagerness to exonerate Cresap, Brantz conveniently ignored much of the evidence Jefferson had gathered, and Brantz too suppressed some evidence, including contemporary accounts that Cresap had been involved in other murders of Natives.

"One may ask who sinned more," wrote Madison's biographer Irving Brant, "Jefferson by suppressing a letter which he knew to be a glossing of the facts, or Brantz Mayer by suppressing the whole mass of contemporary evidence which proved Jefferson guilty of nothing but understatement."

More recently, historian Anthony F. C. Wallace argued provocatively that Jefferson covered up Clark's letter because he wanted to keep the focus on Cresap rather than the broader causes of Lord Dunmore's War. In reality, Cresap was one of many frontiersmen for whom killing Natives was just part of a day's work. Moreover, Wallace stressed, part of that work was on behalf of land speculators back east who included George Washington and Jefferson himself. Better to make Cresap a scapegoat for the war than to admit it was part of a systematic effort to eliminate Natives from the frontier.

And so we are faced—as is so often the case with the man historian Joseph Ellis called the "American sphinx"—with the inconsistencies and ironies of Thomas Jefferson. What seemed at first glance Jefferson's adamant rejection of anti-Indian prejudice turns out on closer inspection to be in some ways a justification of policies and practices that almost wiped out Native Americans. "Jefferson appears both as the scholarly admirer of Indian character, archaeology, and language," Wallace wrote, "and as the planner of cultural genocide, the architect of the removal policy, the surveyor of the Trail of Tears."

How was it possible for one man to hold such contradictory positions? How could one man spend so much time collecting Indian artifacts (he even created an Indian Hall at Monticello, which he stocked with buffalo robes, peace pipes, bows and arrows, wampum, and various items from the Lewis and Clark expedition), recording Indian languages, excavating Indian burial mounds, and deploring the Indians' fate, while doing nothing to prevent—indeed, while actively working to bring about—that fate?

Maybe the contradictions shouldn't so surprise us: this was, after all, the same man who declared all men created equal while himself owning slaves. In the case of Native Americans, Jefferson's dilemma was partly political. As he prepared the appendix to his notes, he was also preparing to run for president, a run that could not succeed without the support of western voters. Jefferson could not afford to portray westerners as land-grabbing killers. Better, again, to blame Cresap and a few murders. Rather than review all the atrocities that led to war, rather than delve into the legal, economic, and military system of which the voters—and Jefferson—were a part, Jefferson chose to praise Logan.

Wallace believed Logan's story held deeper, perhaps subconscious, meanings for Jefferson as well. "Ultimately, in Jefferson's view, the Indian nations would be either civilized and incorporated into mainstream American society or, failing this—as in the prototypical case of Logan's family—'exterminated,'" Wallace wrote. "The Jeffersonian vision of the destiny of the Americas had no place for Indians as Indians." By praising Logan, Jefferson could pay tribute to a dying way of life, but there was no question in his mind that its death was inevitable.

Remarkably, Native culture did not die. Though the Indian population of the Americas is now only about 5 percent of what it was before 1492, Indians have survived into the twenty-first century, and theirs are among the many cultures that make up a more diverse nation than Jefferson or Madison ever imagined. How those diverse cultures can come together as citizens of a single nation remains one of that nation's greatest challenges.

As for Logan, he was not one of the Indian survivors, at least for long. In contrast to Jefferson, we know little about Logan. Even his famous speech comes to us through a translator. (The translator was probably John Gibson, a frontiersman who married into Logan's family and whose wife was among those killed by whites. Gibson later became secretary of the Indiana territory under the Jefferson and Madison administrations.) According to a missionary's report, Logan continued to fight the Americans during the Revolution but became increasingly deranged and in 1780 was killed by his own nephew. That nephew's explanation added another layer of irony to the story of a Native whose life and speech are remembered only because of the writings of those he fought. Logan had to die, the nephew explained, "because he was too great a man to live . . . he talked so strong that nothing could be carried contrary to his opinions."

CHAPTER 22

GEORGE
WASHINGTON

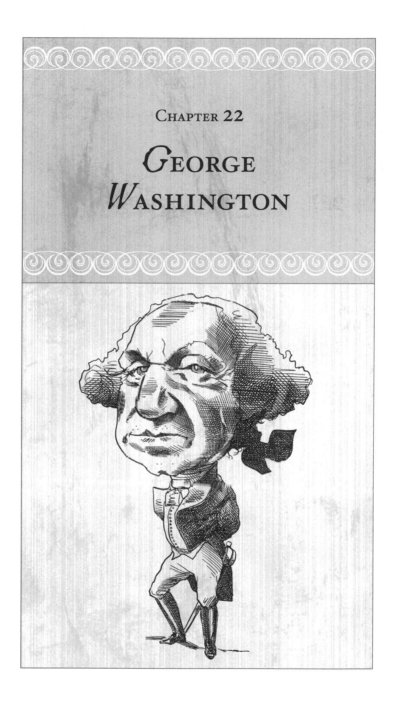

"I can't tell a lie"

GEORGE WASHINGTON'S most celebrated words first appeared in 1806 in the fifth edition of Mason Weems's *Life of Washington*. As Weems told the story, the six-year-old George received a hatchet as a present and immediately set about chopping down everything in his way, including his father's favorite cherry tree.

> The next morning the old gentleman finding out what had befallen his tree . . . came into the house, and with much warmth asked for the mischievous author, declaring at the same time, that he would not have taken five guineas for his tree. Nobody could tell him anything about it. Presently George and his hatchet made their appearance. *George*, said his father, *do you know who killed that beautiful little cherry-tree yonder in the garden?* This was a *tough question*; and George staggered under it for a moment; but quickly recovered himself: and looking at his father, with the sweet face of youth brightened with the inexpressible charm of all-conquering truth, he bravely cried out, *"I can't tell a lie, Pa; you know I can't tell a lie. I did cut it with my hatchet."*

Truth was, in this case, its own reward. Continued Weems:

> *Run to my arms, you dearest boy*, cried his father in transports, run to my arms; glad am I, George, that you killed my tree; for you have paid me for it a thousand fold. Such an act of heroism in my son is more

worth than a thousand trees, though blossomed with silver, and their fruits of purest gold.

Weems, a traveling book salesman and Anglican clergyman, claimed he had heard the story from "an aged lady, who was a distant relative, and when a girl spent much of her time in the family."

From the start, there were plenty of skeptics. An 1800 edition of the *Monthly Magazine and American Review*, referring to an earlier edition of Weems on Washington, called it "as entertaining and edifying matter as can be found in the annals of fanaticism and absurdity." A reviewer for *Blackwood's Edinburgh Magazine* of 1824–1825 concluded there was "not one word of which I believe." Early Washington biographers, including Jared Sparks, whose work appeared between 1834 and 1837, and Washington Irving (1855–1859), made no mention of the cherry tree, and later ones were openly derisory. Wrote biographer William Roscoe Thayer in 1922: "Only those who willfully prefer to deceive themselves need waste time over an imaginary Father of His Country amusing himself with a fictitious cherry-tree and hatchet."

Still, the story wouldn't die. One reason was that historians really didn't know anything about Washington's childhood. "It was this gap that Parson Weems filled up with such slush of plagiarism and piety," wrote biographer Rupert Hughes in 1926. Some tried to fill the gap by treating Washington as if he had been born an adult; John Marshall titled the opening section of his *Life of George Washington* (1804–1807) "The Birth of Mr. Washington." Others focused on the few words the young Washington actually wrote, especially 110 "rules of civility and decent behaviour in company and conversation," which he copied from a translation of a sixteenth-century compilation by

Jesuit scholars. But there's no real evidence these rules were anything more to Washington than homework, and part of their appeal to scholars has admittedly been how funny they sound to modern ears. Just a sampling: "In the presence of others sing not to yourself with a humming noise, nor drum with your fingers or feet" (#4), or "Put not your meat to your mouth with your knife in your hand neither spit forth the stones of any fruit pye upon a dish nor cast anything under the table" (#95).

None of these rules, however entertaining, could match the appeal of the cherry tree, especially to children's writers and Sunday school teachers. Starting with the McGuffey Readers of the nineteenth century, the story found its way into countless children's books. Even those who seemed to know better couldn't resist. "Stories about George Washington as a boy have been retold so often through the years that even though we're not sure they really did happen, they have become a part of the story of America," wrote children's book author Bella Koral in 1954. "And they do tell us something of the kind of boy he was."

Well, no. But they do tell us a great deal about the nation we wanted to be. The cherry tree story was, in some sense, America's creation myth—with George in the role of a more honest Adam and his father as a more forgiving God. By the time George grew up to be president, he would himself be seen as virtually an American god.

"I heard the bullets whistle"

In 1753, when Washington was only twenty-one and a major in the Virginia militia, the colony's governor, Robert Dinwiddie, sent him into the Pennsylvania wilderness. With an interpreter, a scout, and some traders, Washington traveled three hundred miles through hostile Indian and French territory to deliver to the French commander Dinwiddie's message protesting the French presence there. The French predictably refused to leave. Washington's journal of the expedition, which Dinwiddie published in Williamsburg the next year, set him on the road to fame.

In 1754, Washington headed back into the wilderness with about 160 Virginia militiamen and some friendly Iroquois Indians. After building a rough fortification known as Fort Necessity, Washington attacked a French camp, killing about ten Frenchmen and creating a diplomatic incident. Though not officially declared until 1756, the French and Indian War had begun.

"I heard the bullets whistle," an exhilarated Washington wrote his brother after the battle, "and, believe me, there is something charming in the sound."

The French retaliated by sending a far larger force to besiege Fort Necessity, compelling Washington to surrender. He returned to Williamsburg, leaving the Ohio River region in French control.

Washington soon had another opportunity to join the British army. He agreed to serve as aide-de-camp to British General Edward Braddock, who had come to America to lead the campaign against the French. In 1755, in the same territory Washington had failed to capture the year before, Washington "had four bullets through my coat, and two horses shot under me, and yet escaped unhurt." Again, the British forces were defeated, this time with nearly nine hundred British and colonial soldiers wounded or killed, including Braddock.

These early military experiences were notably unsuccessful. But, though Washington's reputation for honesty was still in the future, a reputation for bravery was now firmly established. So in June 1775, when the not-yet-declared independent nation needed a commander in chief, the Continental Congress turned to Washington.

"their marches might be traced by the blood from their feet"

Washington was not a brilliant military strategist, but no one could match his perseverance, and many historians believe that was ultimately the key to winning the Revolution. Nowhere was that more evident than at Valley Forge, twenty-three miles northwest of Philadelphia.

Washington's troops had suffered a series of defeats during late 1777, and Valley Forge was an easy site to defend. It was not, however, an easy site at which to house nearly thirteen thousand men. For starters, there were few buildings, and the men had to live in tents until they could chop down some trees and erect huts. Worse, Congress was slow to allocate any funds for clothes, shoes, food, or medicine, and the army was soon short of everything.

Abilgence Waldo, an army surgeon, described the bleak scene:

> Here comes a soldier; his bare feet are seen through his worn-out shoes, his legs nearly naked from the tattered remains of an only pair of stockings, his breeches not sufficient to cover his nakedness, his shirt hanging in strings, his hair disheveled, his face meager, his whole appearance pictures a person forsaken and discouraged. He comes, and cries with an air of wretchedness and despair, "I am sick, my feet lame, my legs are sore, my body covered with this tormenting itch."

Private Henry Dearborn summed it up this way: "We have not so merry a Christmas."

Washington was irate. "Unless some great and capital change suddenly takes place, this Army must inevitably be reduced to one or other of these three things. Starve, dissolve, or disperse," he wrote Congress in December. "It is a much easier and less distressing thing to draw remonstrances in a comfortable room by a good fire than to occupy a cold bleak hill and sleep under frost and snow without clothes or blankets."

The situation continued to deteriorate, as disease spread through the ranks. The shortage of shoes was so dire that Washington offered ten dollars to anyone who could design a substitute using the rawhide that was still plentiful. By February, Washington ordered the clothing stripped from dead soldiers and distributed to the living. Meanwhile, there was talk in Congress that Washington ought to be relieved of command.

Through it all, Washington persevered, holding his army together with a mix of discipline and inspiration. By April, new supplies and warmer weather had eased conditions, but the winter's travails were still fresh in Washington's mind. He vividly recalled the winter's privations in a letter to John Banister, a Virginian and a member of the Continental Congress:

> To see men without clothes to cover their nakedness — without blankets to lay on, without shoes, by which their marches might be traced by the blood from their feet, and almost as often without provisions as with; marching through frost and snow, and at Christmas taking up their winter quarters within a day's march of the enemy, without a house or hut to cover them till they could be built and submitting to it

without a murmur, is a mark of patience and obedience which in my opinion can scarce be parallelled.

"If their citizens should not be completely free and happy, the fault will be entirely their own"

After Washington's troops, aided by the French army and navy, defeated the British at Yorktown, Virginia, in October 1781, independence seemed—at least in retrospect—inevitable. Not to Washington, however. Hostilities continued in the west, and he had no intention of disbanding his army until a peace treaty was signed. He was also annoyed that Congress showed no signs of keeping its promise to pay soldiers a pension. "The Army, as usual, are without pay," Washington wrote John Armstrong, a delegate to Congress from Pennsylvania, in January 1783, "and a great part of the soldiery without shirts." Perhaps, Washington suggested, Congress felt that the soldiers "had contracted such a habit of encountering distresses and difficulties, and of living without money, that it would be impolitic and injurious to introduce other customs."

Such comments led many to suspect that Washington was planning a military coup. True, he had accepted command of the army in 1775 only, he said, "for the support of the glorious cause" and professing himself not "equal to the command I am honoured with." But cynics could not help but note that as a Virginia delegate to the second Continental Congress Washington had attended wearing the blue and buff uniform of the Fairfax County militia—from his French and Indian War days. This was a fairly blatant statement that he was ready to take command. Many thought of Washington as another Caesar, mouthing support for the republic while preparing to make himself emperor. Among those who thought Washington would never step down was King George III. According to Benjamin West, an American who painted portraits of the royal family, the king was told Washington might retire to his farm. "If he does that," George supposedly responded, "he will be the greatest man in the world."

Whispers of a coup grew louder as Washington's men lost patience with Congress's failure to redeem overdue pay and pension claims. In 1783, an anonymous letter known as the Newburgh Address circulated among Washington's officers. The letter, which came to be known as the Newburgh Address since Washington's headquarters were in Newburgh, New York, warned that "faith has its limits, as well as temper." Joseph Jones, a congressman from Virginia, wrote Washington that "reports are freely circulated here that there are dangerous combinations in the army, and within a few days past it has been said that they are about to declare they will not disband until their demands are complied with."

On March 15, Washington put an end to such talk. Addressing his officers, he took from his pocket a letter and his spectacles, commenting that "I have not only grown gray, but almost blind, in the service of my country." Washington then proceeded to read the letter, which stressed that he had "never left your side one moment," that he had been "the constant companion and witness of your distresses," that he "considered my own military reputation as inseparably connected with that of the army." Finally, he called on their "sacred honor, as you respect the rights of humanity, and as you regard the military and national character of America, to express your utmost horror and detestation of the man who wishes, under any specious pretences, to overturn the liberties of our country, and who wickedly attempts to open the flood gates of civil discord, and deluge our rising empire in blood." Admonished, the officers repudiated the conspirators and expressed their confidence in Congress.

If any doubt remained about Washington's commitment to republicanism, he laid it to rest in his final letter to the states in June 1783. "The citizens of America," he wrote, were "in the most enviable condition" any people had ever experienced. They were "sole lords and proprietors of a vast tract of continent, comprehending all the various soils and climates of the world, and abounding with all the necessaries and conveniences of life." And now, they also possessed "absolute freedom and independency." They are "actors on a most conspicuous theatre, which seems to be peculiarly designed by Providence for the display of human greatness and felicity."

"If their citizens should not be completely free and happy," Washington concluded, "the fault will be entirely their own."

In September, the peace treaty with Britain was signed, and three months later Washington resigned his commission. "Having now finished the work assigned me," he told Congress, "I retire from the great theatre of action."

Washington, it turned out, was not Caesar but Cincinnatus, the Roman hero who returned to his farm after saving the republic. He retired to Mount Vernon, from where he wrote the Marquis de Lafayette, who had been with him at Valley Forge and at Yorktown: "I am become a private citizen on the banks of the Potomac, and under the shadow of my own vine and my own fig tree."

"My movement to the chair of government will be accompanied by feelings not unlike those of a culprit who is going to the place of his execution"

Washington's retirement was short-lived. In May 1787, he was unanimously elected president of the Constitutional Convention. Two years later, under the terms of the new Constitution, he was elected president of the United States. Again, he accepted only amid many professions of reluctance and regret. "My movements to the chair of government," he wrote Henry Knox, who had served under him in the Revolution and would become the first secretary of war, "will be accompanied by feelings not unlike those of a culprit who is going to the place of his execution."

Four years later, he again planned to retire, going so far as to ask James Madison to write a "Valedictory Address." Madison complied but added that he wished Washington would make "one more sacrifice . . . to the desire and interests of your country." Cabinet members Alexander Hamilton and Thomas Jefferson, who disagreed about pretty much everything else, agreed their boss was indispensable. Hamilton called Washington's planned retirement "the greatest evil, that could befall the country at the present juncture." Jefferson argued "North and South will hang together" only "if they have you to hang on." Jefferson acknowledged Washington's desire to retire but explained "there is sometimes an eminence of character in which society have peculiar claims as to control the predilection of the individual." Washington agreed to serve one more term.

In 1796, there would be no changing his mind. This time Washington turned to Hamilton to prepare his farewell. Over the summer Washington and Hamilton exchanged several drafts of what became known as his "Farewell Address." The Address was misnamed; Washington never gave it as an address. Instead, it was published in a Philadelphia newspaper and reprinted in other newspapers across the country. But it was most definitely a farewell, announcing "the resolution I have formed, to decline being considered" for a third term as president.

Much of the Address was devoted to a strong condemnation of the increasing partisanship in American politics. Washington's followers had split into two camps, with Hamilton and John Adams leading what would become the Federalist Party and Jefferson and Madison the Republican Party. Eventually, the two-party system would be seen as a key part of American democracy, since it gave a legitimate role to an organized opposition. Washington, along with most of his contemporaries, did not see it this way. "Your union ought to be considered as a main prop of your liberty," he wrote, "and . . . the love of the one ought to endear to you the preservation of the other." With the prominence in the late twentieth and early twenty-first century of single-issue interest groups and constituencies based on race, ethnicity, gender, and geography, some have again found wisdom in Washington's words.

Perhaps more significant than anything Washington said in the Farewell Address was the departure itself. His talk about wishing only for his vine and fig trees was to some extent an act, for Washington was undeniably ambitious. But by 1796 he was genuinely tired of public service. And his ambition had always been tied not only to his own success but to that of the Revolution. By refusing a third term, Washington proved that he was *not* indispensable, that the American experiment depended on no single man but rather on an entire people. His final farewell defined the American presidency as definitively not a monarchy, securing not only his own legacy but also that of the Revolution.

"entangling alliances with none"

A footnote to the Farewell Address: its most quoted words had to do with foreign policy, urging "peace . . . with all nations" and "entangling alliances with none." Prior to World War I and World War II, isolationists regularly cited these words to buttress their case. They were not entirely wrong to cite the Farewell Address, which did urge Americans to "steer clear of permanent alliances with any portion of the foreign world." The words "entangling alliances," however, appear nowhere in the Farewell Address; they are actually from Thomas Jefferson's inaugural address of 1801. These were no more Washington's words than "I can't tell a lie."

"First in war, first in peace, first in the hearts of his countrymen"

Washington's apotheosis was by no means the work of Weems alone. "Had he lived in the days of idolatry," wrote the *Pennsylvania Journal* in 1777, "he had been worshipped as a god." "Thy fame is of sweeter perfume than Arabian spices in the gardens of Persia," said Ezra Stiles, the president of Yale University in 1783. "Listening angels shall catch the odor, waft it to heaven, and perfume the universe!"

Washington's death in 1799 brought forth a torrent of praise, as the new nation wondered whether it could survive without him. Of all the eulogies, the best remembered was that of Henry Lee. "First in war, first in peace, first in the hearts of his countrymen," said Lee, "he was second to none in the humble and endearing scenes of private life. . . . his example was as edifying to all around him, as were the effects of that example lasting."

Lee's own reputation as a Revolutionary hero was not lasting. The father of Robert E. Lee and the cousin of Richard Henry Lee, Henry Lee's lightning-quick cavalry attacks on the British earned him the name of "Light-Horse Harry." He served briefly as governor of Virginia and was elected to Congress in 1799, enabling him to give the eulogy at Congress' memorial service for Washington. Alas, unsuccessful speculation in real estate and other dubious investments forced Lee to sell off much of his land and eventually landed him in jail. He later fled to the West Indies and died in exile.

Yet Lee's tribute—and Washington's reputation— would, deservedly, endure. Washington's military victories against the odds; his unifying leadership during the nation's early years; his willingness, repeatedly, to relinquish power and thus prove a republic could survive: these earned him his place in the hearts of his countrymen, then and now. Wrote historian Joseph Ellis:

> Benjamin Franklin was wiser than Washington; Alexander Hamilton was more brilliant; John Adams was better read; Thomas Jefferson was more intellectually sophisticated; James Madison was more politically astute. Yet each and all of these prominent figures acknowledged that Washington was their unquestioned superior. Within the gallery of greats so often mythologized and capitalized as Founding Fathers, Washington was . . . the Foundingest Father of them all.

Chapter 23

Phillis Wheatley

"In every human breast, God has implanted a principle, which we call love of freedom"

IN 1772, a poet wrote the following lines celebrating the arrival, which she hoped was imminent, of American freedom:

No more, *America*, in mournful strain
Of wrongs, and grievance unredress'd complain,
No longer shall thou dread the iron chain,
Which wanton *Tyranny* with lawless hand
Had made, and with it meant t'enslave the land.

The patriot poet was Phillis Wheatley, a seventeen-year-old slave girl. Kidnapped from her native Africa, she had arrived in Boston aboard the schooner, the *Phillis*, in 1761 at about the age of seven. She had been bought by Susannah and John Wheatley, of Boston, and put to work as a house servant. According to descendants of the Wheatleys, they had sensed her talents soon after, when they found her writing English letters on a wall with a piece of chalk. The Wheatleys took upon themselves the child's education, encouraged her to read and write, and then determined to help her publish a collection of poetry.

Such were the prejudices of the day, however, that no publisher would take on the work, at least partly because they didn't believe a Negro could have written poetry. In October 1772, therefore, the Wheatleys arranged for "the most respectable characters in Boston" to quiz the child and decide whether she was, in fact, the poet. These included Governor Thomas Hutchinson of Massachusetts and John Hancock, who would be the first man to sign the Declaration of Independence. They concluded that the poems were "written by Phillis, a young Negro girl, who was but a few years since brought an uncultivated barbarian from Africa, and has ever since been, and now is, under the disadvantage of serving as a slave in a family in this town."

The collection was published in 1773, though in England, not America. The Wheatleys allowed her to go to London for the publication. There she was a celebrity, meeting with English gentry and abolitionists as well as Benjamin Franklin. When she returned to America, the Wheatleys freed her. Another signer of the Declaration, Benjamin Rush, praised her "singular genius and accomplishments," which "not only do honour to her sex, but to human nature." Wheatley wrote a poem honoring George Washington, and he thanked her for the "elegant lines" and told her that "however undeserving I may be of such encomium and panegyric, the style and manner exhibit a striking proof of your poetical talents."

One founding father who most decidedly did not appreciate Wheatley's talents was Thomas Jefferson. "Misery is often the parent of the most affecting touches in poetry," he conceded in *Notes on the State of Virginia*. "Among blacks is misery enough, God knows, but not poetry. . . . Their love is ardent, but it kindles the senses only, not the imagination. Religion, indeed, has produced a Phyllis Whately [sic]; but it could not produce a poet. The compositions under her name are below the dignity of criticism."

Wheatley's limitations, Jefferson explained, did not stem from her condition as a slave. The slaves of the ancient Romans were often "their rarest artists." Lest there be any doubt of his meaning, Jefferson added: "But they were of the race of whites."

Among modern critics, Wheatley's most vehement detractors have not been whites but blacks. Many criticized Wheatley for the very trait for which she'd once been praised: her mastery of neoclassical forms. Amiri Baraka, the poet and critic, wrote that Wheatley's "pleasant imitations of eighteenth-century English poetry are far and, finally, ludicrous departures from the huge black voices that splintered southern nights." Novelist Alice Walker described Wheatley's poetry as "stiff, struggling, ambivalent." Searching for an authentic African American voice, critics found in Wheatley nothing but "an early Boston Aunt Jemima."

Critics also questioned why a black slave would embrace the cause of the American patriots, who were after all her people's oppressors. They found especially offensive "On Being Brought from Africa to America," a poem Wheatley wrote in 1768 when she was about fourteen years old. The poem had only eight lines:

'Twas mercy brought me from my *Pagan* land,
Taught my benighted soul to understand
That there's a God, that there's a *Saviour* too:
Once I redemption neither sought nor knew
Some view our sable race with scornful eye,
"Their colour is a diabolic die."
Remember, *Christians*, *Negros*, black as *Cain*,
May be refin'd, and join th' angelic train.

"This . . . has been the most reviled poem in African-American literature," wrote historian and critic Henry

Louis Gates, Jr. "To speak in such glowing terms about the 'mercy' manifested by the slave trade was not exactly going to endear Miss Wheatley to black power advocates in the 1960s."

True enough. Wheatley was grateful to have found Christianity, and she came to it via slavery. Still, it's worth noting that her concept of Christianity was one in which blacks as well as whites could "join th' angelic train." Moreover, as scholars including Gates, Vincent Carretta, William Robinson, and John Shields have pointed out, many of Wheatley's other poems expressed antislavery sentiments. For example, in the 1772 poem "To the Right Honourable William, Earl of Dartmouth" (excerpted at the beginning of this chapter), she wrote of the misery that followed her being "snatch'd from Afric's fancy'd happy seat":

> What pangs excruciating must molest,
> What sorrows labour in my parent's breast?
> Steel'd was that soul and by no misery mov'd
> That from a father seiz'd his babe belov'd:
> Such, such my case. And can then but pray
> Others may never feel tyrannic sway?

The image in that poem of an "iron chain" and the references to the "wanton Tyranny" meant "t' enslave the land" must have held special resonance for a slave poet. Similar images abound in Wheatley's patriotic poems. In her 1768 poem, "America," for example, the child of "great Brittania" (the American colonies) "weeps afresh to feel this Iron chain." One can't help but read many of Wheatley's poems about American freedom as, also, calls to end slavery.

Wheatley's antislavery sentiments were most explicit in her letters. Of these, the best known is her February 1774 letter to the Reverend Samson Occom, a converted Indian minister. "In every human breast," Wheatley wrote, "God has implanted a principle, which we call love of freedom; it is impatient of oppression, and pants for deliverance; and by the leave of our modern Egyptians I will assert, that the same principle lives in us." In the same letter, Wheatley made clear what she thought of American slaveholders who complained about British tyranny. "How well the cry for liberty, and the reverse disposition for the exercise of oppressive power over others agree," she wrote, "I humbly think it does not require the penetration of a philosopher to determine."

Certainly Wheatley, even after gaining her freedom, understood the difficulties of being a black woman in eighteenth-century America. She never succeeded in finding a publisher for a second volume of poetry. She had three children, none of whom outlived her. She survived by cleaning houses until 1784, when she died, alone and impoverished, at the age of thirty.

CHAPTER 24

JAMES WILSON

"We the people"

WHAT ALEXANDER Hamilton referred to as "the imbecility of our government" was, by 1787, painfully clear. Under the Articles of Confederation, the agreement between the states formed during the Revolution, the federal government was unable to pay its debts, enforce its treaties, or put down uprisings in Massachusetts, Pennsylvania, and Virginia. Often, Congress couldn't even muster a quorum.

To fix the Articles, fifty-five delegates from twelve states (Rhode Island declined to participate) gathered in Philadelphia that summer. The eminent gathering included Benjamin Franklin, Alexander Hamilton, James Madison, and George Washington. These were men of "ability, weight, and experience," said John Adams. "An assembly of demigods," agreed Thomas Jefferson.

After months of deliberating, the Convention unveiled not revised articles but a new constitution. The document's Preamble set forth its intent: "We, the People of the United States, in Order to form a more perfect union, establish justice, ensure domestic tranquility, provide for the common defence, promote the general welfare, and secure the blessings of liberty to ourselves and our posterity, do ordain and establish this Constitution for the United States of America."

Since the Convention took place behind closed doors—the delegates went so far as to nail shut the windows of the meeting room—there are many details about how the Constitution was composed that we don't know.

Naturally, historians have pored over the notes and drafts that emerged. The Preamble, we thus suspect, came from the quill of one of the lesser (or at least lesser-known) demigods, James Wilson of Pennsylvania. Wilson was one of just six men to sign both the Constitution and the Declaration of Independence.

For the author of words as radically democratic as the Preamble's, Wilson hardly seemed a man of the people. Back in 1776, he approached independence cautiously, at least until the Pennsylvania legislature made its support clear. In 1779, his opposition to wartime price controls prompted a mob to attack his house, leaving six dead. "His lofty carriage," the Philadelphia *Independent Gazetteer* said of Wilson, "indicates the lofty mind that animates him, a mind able to conceive and perform great things, but which unfortunately can see nothing great out of the pale of power and worldly grandeur."

Wilson was one of five men the Convention assigned, on July 26th, to a "committee of detail" that would draft a constitution based on the resolutions passed in the previous weeks. A draft of the Preamble was found among Wilson's papers and in Wilson's handwriting. It reads: "We the People of and the States of New Hampshire, Massachusetts. . . ." It goes on to list thirteen states. On the draft, the word "and," is crossed out, so that the Preamble begins: "We the People of the States. . . ."

The deletion was crucial. Wilson not only approached the document's final wording but also stressed its democratic premise. The states may have sent the delegates to the Convention, but it was the people of the states who were the basis of the Constitution's legitimacy.

Wilson did not, of course, invent the idea of "the people." Nor can we know for sure, despite his handwriting, that these words weren't suggested by some other member of the committee. Still, Wilson is the likely choice. Despite his "lofty carriage," Wilson was as committed to popular sovereignty as any delegate to the Convention. The words of the Preamble echo through Wilson's other writings and speeches. Wilson wrote the draft to the 1776 Pennsylvania constitution, which opened with "We, the representatives of the freemen of Pennsylvania . . . do . . . ordain, declare and establish the following . . . Constitution."

Wilson also led the fight to ratify the Constitution. At the Pennsylvania Convention of 1787, Wilson—without claiming its authorship—repeatedly drove home the significance of the Constitution's opening. "This single sentence in the Preamble," he proclaimed, "is tantamount to a volume and contains the essence of all the bills of rights that have been or can be devised; for, it establishes, at once, that in the great article of government, the people have a right to do what they please."

Wilson then compared the Constitution to Britain's "boasted Magna Charta." "The very words of that celebrated instrument declare them to be the gift or grant of the king. . . . But here, sir, the fee simple of freedom and government is declared to be in the people, and it is an inheritance with which they will not part."

The work of Wilson and his fellow Federalists paid off, with eleven states (including Pennsylvania) ratifying the Constitution by mid-1788. Appropriately, Wilson spoke at a celebration in Philadelphia. "You have heard of Sparta, of Athens, and of Rome," he told a crowd of twenty thousand. Wilson continued:

> You have heard of their admired constitutions, and of their high-prized freedom. . . . But did they . . . ever furnish, to the astonished world, an exhibition similar to that which we now contemplate? Were their

constitutions framed by those, who were appointed
for that purpose, by the people? After they were
framed, were they submitted to the consideration of
the people? . . . Were they to stand or fall by the people's approving or rejecting vote?

Did the delegates to the Constitutional Convention
intend to create so democratic a government? That's a
question historians have debated in the centuries since
1788. Many noted that the founding fathers were all white
and generally rich men and that "the people" of the Constitution clearly didn't include slaves or women. Others
argued that the Constitution was more republican than
democratic, in that it gave power to the people's representatives rather than the people themselves. The founders'
own words provided plenty of evidence for this view;
Edmund Randolph, for example, spoke of "the turbulence
and follies of democracy," and even Madison worried that
in "all very numerous assemblies . . . passion never fails to
wrest the scepter from reason."

The antidemocratic character of the Convention was the
central theme of Charles Beard's influential 1913 book, *An
Economic Interpretation of the Constitution of the United States.*
Beard maintained that the supporters of the Constitution
were primarily motivated by financial interests. By creating a
stronger central government with more taxing power, the
Federalists would increase the value of the certificates of
public debt and public currency that many of them held.
Wilson, for example, had significant banking interests.

Beard's arguments resonated in the context of the
early twentieth century. Compared to the Bolsheviks in
Russia, America's founding fathers hardly seemed revolutionary. In the second half of the twentieth century, how-

ever, historians such as Forrest McDonald discredited much of Beard's economic analysis. Gordon Wood's acclaimed 1969 book, *The Creation of the American Republic*, brought back to the foreground the ideas, as opposed to economic interests, of the founders. Wood demonstrated that the founders, in embracing republican principles, were also embracing democratic ones. He quoted, among others, Wilson, who argued that the executive and judicial branches of the government were as much "the child of the people" as the legislative branch. The Constitution was "purely democratical," Wilson said, because "all authority of every kind is derived by representation from the people."

In the context of the eighteenth century, the Constitution was indeed a democratic document. Compare the government it envisioned to others of the time, ruled by kings and czars and sultans. Even the English Constitution, however admirable, had never been written down and voted on by the British people. The Articles of Confederation were ratified by state legislatures, none of which submitted the document to any sort of referendum. In contrast, the Constitution of 1787 was ratified, though not by the people themselves, by conventions elected by a broader, less-propertied class of citizens than previous elections in America had allowed. And when those people demanded the Constitution be changed—most immediately by adding a Bill of Rights—that's exactly what happened. Slaves and women, too, would eventually benefit from amendments to the Constitution, albeit not until 1865 and 1920, respectively.

As for Wilson, if he had any of his own interests in mind when he penned "the people," it brought him neither fame nor fortune. Few Americans, even those who know his words, know his name. Though he was appointed to the Supreme Court, his speculations landed him deeply in debt, and his role on the court was limited by his fear that, if he entered any of several states, he would land in debtors' prison. He died in 1798 while hiding from his creditors in the Edenton, North Carolina, home of his fellow Supreme Court justice, James Iredell.

BIBLIOGRAPHY

ABIGAIL ADAMS

Remember the Ladies

Akers, Charles W. *Abigail Adams*. New York: Pearson Longman, 2007.
Butterfield, L. H., ed. *Adams Family Correspondence*. Cambridge, Mass.: Belknap, 1963.
Levin, Phyllis Lee. *Abigail Adams*. New York: St. Martin's, 2001.
Nagel, Paul C. *The Adams Women*. New York: Oxford University Press, 1987.
———. *The Lees of Virginia*. New York: Oxford University Press, 1990.
Norton, Mary Beth. *Liberty's Daughters*. Boston: Little, Brown, 1980.
Taylor, Robert J., ed. *Papers of John Adams*. Cambridge, Mass.: Belknap, 1977.
Withey, Lynne. *Dearest Friend*. New York: Free Press, 1981.

JOHN ADAMS

Facts are stubborn things

the most insignificant office that ever the invention of man contrived

The Revolution was in the minds
and hearts of the people

Thomas Jefferson survives

Adams, Charles Francis, ed. *The Works of John Adams* (10 volumes). Boston: Little, Brown, 1856.
Diggins, John Patrick. *John Adams*. New York: Times Books, 2003.
Ellis, Joseph J. *Passionate Sage*. New York: W. W. Norton, 1993.
Grant, James. *John Adams*. New York: Farrar, Straus and Giroux, 2005.
McCullough, David. *John Adams*. New York: Simon & Schuster, 2001.
Wood, Gordon S. *Revolutionary Characters*. New York: Penguin, 2006.
Zall, Paul M., ed. *Adams on Adams*. Lexington: University Press of Kentucky, 2004.
Zobel, Hiller. *The Boston Massacre*. New York: W. W. Norton, 1970.

ANONYMOUS

E Pluribus Unum

Yankee Doodle went to town

Deutsch, Monroe E. "*E Pluribus Unum*." *The Classical Journal* 18, no. 7 (1923): 387–407.
LeMay, J. A. Leo. "The American Origins of 'Yankee Doodle.'" *William & Mary Quarterly* 33, no. 3 (1976): 435–64.
Murray, Stuart. *America's Song*. Bennington, Vt.: Images from the Past, 1999.
Oxford English Dictionary Online. Oxford: Oxford University Press, 2008.
Sonneck, Oscar. *Report on "The Star-Spangled Banner," "Hail Columbia," "America," & "Yankee Doodle."* Washington, D.C.: Government Printing Office, 1909.
United States Department of State. *The Great Seal of the United States*. Washington, D.C.: Bureau of Public Affairs, 2003.

John Dickinson

By uniting we stand, by dividing we fall

United, we stand—Divided, we fall

Bailyn, Bernard. *Pamphlets of the American Revolution.* Vol. 1. Cambridge, Mass.: Harvard University Press, 1965.
Flower, Milton E. *John Dickinson.* Charlottesville: University Press of Virginia, 1983.
Ford, Paul Leicester, ed. *The Writings of John Dickinson.* Vol. 1. Philadelphia: Historical Society of Pennsylvania, 1895.
Jacobson, David L. *John Dickinson and the Revolution in Pennsylvania.* Berkeley: University of California Press, 1965.

Olaudah Equiano

The shrieks of the women, and the groans of the dying

Carretta, Vincent. *Equiano the African.* Athens: University of Georgia Press, 2005.
Equiano, Olaudah. *The Interesting Narrative and Other Writings.* Edited by Vincent Carretta. New York: Penguin, 2003 (originally published in 1789).
Hochschild, Adam. *Bury the Chains.* Boston: Houghton Mifflin, 2005.
Walvin, James. *An African's Life.* New York: Cassell, 1998.

Benjamin Franklin

Early to bed and early to rise

Let the experiment be made

Join, or Die

Don't tread on me

We must . . . all hang together, or most assuredly we shall all hang separately

A republic if you can keep it

Chaplin, Joyce. *The First Scientific American*. New York: Basic Books, 2006.

Force, Peter. *American Archives*. 1837–1853. 4th ser., V, p. 568.

Gaustad, Edwin S. *Benjamin Franklin*. New York: Oxford University Press, 2006.

Godbold, E. Stanly, Jr. *Christopher Gadsden and the American Revolution*. Knoxville: University of Tennessee Press, 1982.

Isaacson, Walter. *Benjamin Franklin*. New York: Simon & Schuster, 2003.

Mieder, Wolfgang. *Proverbs Are Never Out of Season*. New York: Oxford University Press, 1993.

Talbott, Page, ed. *Benjamin Franklin*. New Haven, Conn.: Yale University Press, 2005.

Walsh, Richard, ed. *The Writings of Christopher Gadsden*. Columbia: University of South Carolina Press, 1966.

Wood, Gordon S. *The Americanization of Benjamin Franklin*. New York: Penguin, 2004.

NATHAN HALE

*I only regret that I have but one life
to lose for my country*

Cray, Robert E., Jr. "The Revolutionary Spy as Hero," *Connecticut History* 38, no. 2 (1999): 85–104.

Donnelly, F. K. "A Possible Source for Nathan Hale's Dying Words." *William and Mary Quarterly*, 3rd ser., 42, no. 3 (1985): 394–96.

Kammen, Michael. *A Season of Youth*. New York: Knopf, 1978.

Mooney, Richard E. "One Life to Lose in Four Places." *New-York Journal of American History* 66, no. 1 (2005): 43–47.

Rose, Alexander. *Washington's Spies*. New York: Bantam, 2006.

ALEXANDER HAMILTON

I never expect to see a perfect work from imperfect man

Your people is a great beast

Ambrose, Douglas and Robert W. T. Martin, eds. *The Many Faces of Alexander Hamilton*. New York: New York University Press, 2006.

Brookhiser, Richard. *Alexander Hamilton, American*. New York: Free Press, 1999.

Chernow, Ron. *Alexander Hamilton*. New York: Penguin, 2004.

Ellis, Joseph J. *Founding Brothers*. New York: Knopf, 2001.

Fleming, Thomas. *Duel*. New York: Basic, 1999.

Hamilton, Alexander, James Madison, and John Jay. *The Federalist*. Edited by Terence Ball. New York: Cambridge University Press, 2003.

Kennedy, Roger G. *Burr, Hamilton, and Jefferson*. New York: Oxford, 2000.

Knott, Stephen F. *Alexander Hamilton & the Persistence of Myth*. Lawrence: University Press of Kansas, 2002.

Wood, Gordon. *Revolutionary Characters*. New York: Penguin, 2006.

JOHN HANCOCK

I write so that King George III may read without his spectacles

Allan, Herbert S. *John Hancock*. New York: Macmillan, 1948.

Boyd, Julian P., ed. *The Papers of Thomas Jefferson*. Vol. 1. Princeton, N.J.: Princeton University Press, 1950.

Brandes, Paul D. *John Hancock's Life and Speeches*. Lanham, Md.: Scarecrow Press, 1996.

Fowler, William M. *The Baron of Beacon Hill*. Boston: Houghton Mifflin, 1980.

Hazelton, J. H. *The Declaration of Independence*. New York: Da Capo Press, 1970 (reprint of 1906 edition).

Maier, Pauline. *American Scripture*. New York: Alfred A. Knopf, 1997.

Unger, Harlow Giles. *John Hancock*. New York: John Wiley & Sons, 2000.

Warren, Charles. "Fourth of July Myths." *William and Mary Quarterly*, 3rd ser., 2, no. 3 (1945): 237–72.

Watson, John F. *Annals of Philadelphia and Pennsylvania in the Olden Time*. Philadelphia: Elijah Thomas, 1857.

PATRICK HENRY

If this be treason, make the most of it

Give me liberty, or give me death

Carson, Jane. *Patrick Henry, Prophet of the Revolution*. Williamsburg: Virginia Independence Bicentennial Commission, 1979.

McCants, David A. *Patrick Henry, The Orator*. New York: Greenwood, 1990.

Mayer, Henry. *A Son of Thunder*. New York: Franklin Watts, 1986.

Mayo, Bernard. "The Enigma of Patrick Henry." *Virginia Quarterly Review* 35, no. 2 (1959): 176–95.

Tyler, Moses Coit. *Patrick Henry*. New York: Chelsea House, 1980.

Wirt, William. *The Life of Patrick Henry*. Freeport, N.Y.: Books for Libraries, 1970 (reprint of 1836 edition).

Thomas Jefferson

We hold these truths to be self-evident

a wall of separation between church and state

I like a little rebellion now and then

*a government without newspapers or
newspapers without a government*

We have the wolf by the ears

Is it the Fourth?

Appleby, Joyce. *Thomas Jefferson*. New York: Times Books, 2003.

Boyd, Julian P., ed. *The Papers of Thomas Jefferson*. Princeton, N.J.: Princeton University Press, 1950.

Ellis, Joseph J. *American Sphinx*. New York: Alfred A. Knopf, 1997.

———. *Founding Brothers*. New York: Alfred A. Knopf, 2001.

Gaustad, Edwin S. *Sworn on the Altar of God*. Grand Rapids, Mich.: William B. Eerdmans, 1996.

Hazelton, John H. *The Declaration of Independence*. New York: Da Capo Press, 1970 (originally published in 1906).

Levy, Leonard W. *Jefferson and Civil Liberties*. Cambridge, Mass.: Belknap, 1963.

Maier, Pauline. *American Scripture*. New York: Alfred A. Knopf, 1997.

Malone, Dumas. *Jefferson the Virginian*. Vol. 1 of *Jefferson and His Time*. Boston: Little, Brown, 1948.

Miller, John Chester. *The Wolf by the Ears*. New York: Free Press, 1977.
Randall, Willard Sterne. *Thomas Jefferson*. New York: Henry Holt, 1993.
Radbill, Samuel X., ed. *The Autobiographical Ana of Robley Dunglison, M.D.* Philadelphia: American Philosophical Society, 1963.
Wills, Garry, *Inventing America*. New York: Doubleday, 1978.

JOHN PAUL JONES

I have not yet begun to fight

Callo, Joseph. *John Paul Jones*. Annapolis, Md.: Naval Institute Press, 2006.
Morison, Samuel Eliot. *John Paul Jones*. Boston: Little, Brown, 1959.
Thomas, Evan. *John Paul Jones*. New York: Simon & Schuster, 2003.
Vansisttart, Peter. *John Paul Jones*. London: Robson, 2004.
Walsh, John Evangelist. *Night on Fire*. New York: McGraw-Hill, 1978.

FRANCIS SCOTT KEY

O! say can you see

In God is our Trust

Hickey, Donald. R. *Don't Give Up the Ship*. Urbana: University of Illinois Press, 2006.
Molotsky, Irvin. *The Flag, the Poet and the Song*. New York: Dutton, 2001.
Sonneck, Oscar George Theodore. *"The Star Spangled Banner."* Washington, D.C.: Government Printing Office, 1914.
Taylor, Lonn. *The Star-Spangled Banner*. New York: Abrams, 2000.
U.S. Department of the Treasury. At www.treas.gov/education/fact-sheets/currency/in-god-we-trust.html.

JAMES MADISON

If men were angels, no government would be necessary

Congress shall make no law

Amar, Akhil Reed. *America's Constitution*. New York: Random House, 2005.

——. *The Bill of Rights*. New Haven, Conn.: Yale University Press, 1998.

Banning, Lance. *The Sacred Fire of Liberty*. Ithaca, N.Y.: Cornell University Press, 1995.

Bernstein, Richard. *Are We to Be a Nation?* Cambridge, Mass.: Harvard University Press, 1987.

Brant, Irving. *The Fourth President*. Indianapolis: Bobbs-Merrill, 1970.

Cerami, Charles. *Young Patriots*. Naperville, Ill.: Sourcebooks, 2005.

Hamilton, Alexander, James Madison, and John Jay. *The Federalist*. Edited by Terence Ball. New York: Cambridge University Press, 2003.

Labunski, Richard. *James Madison and the Struggle for the Bill of Rights*. New York: Oxford University Press, 2006.

Nedelsky, Jennifer. *Private Property and the Limits of American Constitutionalism*. Chicago: The University of Chicago Press, 1990.

Rakove, Jack N. *James Madison and the Creation of the American Republic*. New York: Pearson Longman, 2007.

Wood, Gordon S. *Revolutionary Characters*. New York: Penguin, 2006.

JOHN MARSHALL

An act of the legislature, repugnant to the Constitution, is void

The government of the Union is, emphatically and truly,
a government of the people

The people made the Constitution,
and the people can unmake it

Cranch, William. *Reports of Cases Argued and Adjudged in the Supreme Court of the United States*. New York: John Conrad, 1804–1817.

Hobson, Charles F. *The Great Chief Justice*. Lawrence: University Press of Kansas, 1996.
Kramer, Larry D. *The People Themselves*. New York: Oxford University Press, 2004.
Newmyer, R. Kent. *John Marshall and the Heroic Age of the Supreme Court*. Baton Rouge: Louisiana State University Press, 2001.
Robarge, David. *A Chief Justice's Progress*. Westport, Conn.: Greenwood Press, 2000.
Smith, Jean Edward. *John Marshall*. New York: Henry Holt, 1996.
Stites, Francis N. *John Marshall*. Boston: Little, Brown, 1981.
Wheaton, Henry. *Reports of Cases Argued and Adjudged in the Supreme Court*. Philadelphia: Matthew Carey, 1816–1827.

GEORGE MASON

*All men are by nature equally free
and independent*

Broadwater, Jeff. *George Mason*. Chapel Hill: University of North Carolina Press, 2006.
Miller, Helen Hill. *George Mason*. Chapel Hill: University of North Carolina Press, 1975.
Selby, John. *The Revolution in Virginia*. Williamsburg, Va.: Colonial Williamsburg Foundation, 1988.
Rutland, Robert A. *George Mason*. Williamsburg, Va.: Colonial Williamsburg Foundation, 1961.
——. *George Mason and the War for Independence*. Williamsburg: Virginia Independence Bicentennial Commission, 1976.
——, ed. *The Papers of George Mason*. Chapel Hill. University of North Carolina Press, 1970.
Tarter, Brent, ed. *Revolutionary Virginia: The Road to Independence*. Vol. vii. Charlottesville: University Press of Virginia, 1983.

JAMES OTIS

*Taxation without representation is tyranny
No taxation without representation*

Adams, Charles Francis. *The Works of John Adams* (10 volumes). Freeport, N.Y.: Books for Libraries Press, 1969 (originally published 1850–1856).

Bailyn, Bernard. *The Ideological Origins of the American Revolution.* Cambridge, Mass.: Harvard University Press, 1967.
——, ed. *Pamphlets of the American Revolution.* Vol. 1. Cambridge, Mass.: Harvard University Press, 1965.
Breen, T. H. "Subjecthood and Citizenship." *New England Quarterly* 71, no. 3 (1998): 378–403.
Corrigan, John. *The Hidden Balance.* New York: Cambridge University Press, 1987.
Ferguson, James R. "Reason in Madness." *William and Mary Quarterly,* 3rd. ser., 36, no. 2 (1979): 194–214.
Galvin, John R. *Three Men of Boston.* New York: Thomas Y. Crowell Company, 1976.
Mood, Fulmer. "Jonathan Mayhew." In *Dictionary of American Biography.* Vol. 12. New York: Scribner's, 1933, pp. 4454–55.
Morison, Samuel Eliot. "James Otis." In *Dictionary of American Biography.* Vol. 14. New York: Scribner's, 1981, pp. 101–5.
Samuelson, Richard A. "The Constitutional Sanity of James Otis." *Review of Politics* 61, no. 3 (1999): 493–523.
Shipton, Clifford K. *Sibley's Harvard Graduates.* Vol. 11. Boston: Massachusetts Historical Society, 1960, pp. 247–87 ("James Otis") and pp. 440–69 ("Jonathan Mayhew").
Tudor, William. *The Life of James Otis.* Boston: Wells and Lilly, 1823.
Waters, John J., Jr. *The Otis Family.* Chapel Hill: University of North Carolina Press, 1968.
Wood, Gordon. *Creation of the American Republic.* Chapel Hill: University of North Carolina Press, 1969.
Worth, L. Kinvin and Hiller B. Zobel, eds. *Legal Papers of John Adams.* Cambridge, Mass.: Harvard University Press, 1965.

THOMAS PAINE

We have it in our power to begin the world over again

These are the times that try men's souls

Collins, Paul. *The Trouble with Tom.* New York: Bloomsbury, 2005.
Foner, Eric. *Tom Paine and Revolutionary America.* New York: Oxford University Press, 1976.

Kaye, Harvey. *Thomas Paine and the Promise of America*. New York: Hill and Wang, 2005.

Keane, John. *Tom Paine*. Boston: Little, Brown, 1995.

Liell, Scott. *46 Pages*. Philadelphia: Running Press, 2003.

Nelson, Craig. *Thomas Paine*. New York: Viking, 2006.

Paine, Thomas. *Common Sense and Other Writings*. Edited and with an introduction by Gordon S. Wood. New York: Modern Library, 2003.

WILLIAM PRESCOTT

Don't fire till you see the whites of their eyes

Bell, J. L. "Who Said, 'Don't Fire Till You See the Whites of Their Eyes?'" and "Who Coined the Phrase 'Till You See the Whites of Their Eyes'?" At boston1775.blogspot.com/2007/06.

Brooks, Victor. *The Boston Campaign*. Conshohocken, Pa.: Combined Pub., 1999.

Commager, Henry Steele and Richard B. Morris. *The Spirit of Seventy-Six*. New York: Harper & Row, 1975.

French, Allen. *The First Year of the American Revolution*. New York: Octagon, 1968 (originally published in 1934).

Frothingham, Richard, Jr. *History of the Siege of Boston*. Boston: Charles C. Little and James Brown, 1851.

Ketchum, Richard M. *Decisive Day*. New York: Doubleday, 1974.

Middlekauff, Robert. *The Glorious Cause*. New York: Oxford University Press, 2005.

Swett, Samuel. *History of Bunker Hill Battle*. Boston: Munroe and Francis, 1826 (first edition 1818).

Weems, Mason L. *The Life of Washington*, ed. by Marcus Cunliffe. Cambridge, Mass.: Harvard University Press, 1962.

Hale, Edward E. "The Siege of Boston." In *The Memorial History of Boston*. Vol. 3, ed. by Justin Winsor. Boston: James R. Osgood, 1881.

Winsor, Justin, ed. *Narrative and Critical History of America*. Boston: Houghton Mifflin, 1887.

PAUL REVERE

One, if by land, and two, if by sea
The British are coming

Fischer, David Hackett. *Paul Revere's Ride*. New York: Oxford University Press, 1994.

Revere, Paul. *Paul Revere's Three Accounts of His Famous Ride*. Boston: Massachusetts Historical Society, 1968.

Triber, Jayne E. *A True Republican*. Amherst: University of Massachusetts, 1998.

TACHNEDORUS

Who is there to mourn for Logan? Not one

Brant, Irving. *James Madison*. Indianapolis, Ind.: Bobbs-Merrill, 1941.

Jefferson, Thomas. *Notes on the State of Virginia*. New York: Penguin, 1999.

Wallace, Anthony F. C. *Jefferson and the Indians*. Cambridge, Mass: Belknap, 1999.

GEORGE WASHINGTON

I can't tell a lie

I heard the bullets whistle

their marches might be traced by the blood from their feet

If their citizens should not be completely free and happy, the fault will be entirely their own

My movement to the chair of government will be accompanied by feelings not unlike those of a culprit who is going to the place of his execution

entangling alliances with none

First in war, first in peace, first in the hearts of his countrymen

Brookhiser, Richard. *Founding Father*. New York: Free Press, 1996.

Burns, James MacGregor and Susan Dunn. *George Washington*. New York: Times Books, 2004.

Chadwick, Bruce. *George Washington's War*. Naperville, Ill.: Sourcebooks, 2005.

Crutchfield, James A. *George Washington*. New York: Forge, 2005
MacGregor, James and Susan Dunn. *George Washington*. New York: Times Books, 2004.
Ellis, Joseph J. *Founding Brothers*. New York: Knopf, 2001.
——. *His Excellency*. New York: Knopf, 2004.
Flexner, James Thomas. *Washington*. Boston: Little, Brown, 1974.
Freeman, Douglas Southall. *George Washington*. New York: Scribner's, 1948–1951.
Longmore, Paul K. *The Invention of George Washington*. Charlottesville: University Press of Virginia, 1999.
Marling, Karal Ann. *George Washington Slept Here*. Cambridge, Mass.: Harvard University Press, 1988.
Royster, Charles. *Light-Horse Harry Lee & the Legacy of the American Revolution*. New York: Cambridge University Press, 1981.
Schwartz, Barry. *George Washington*. New York: Free Press, 1987.
Weems, Mason L. *The Life of Washington*. Edited by Marcus Cunliffe. Cambridge, Mass.: Harvard University Press, 1962.
Wiencek, Henry. *An Imperfect God*. New York: Farrar, Straus and Giroux, 2003.
Wills, Garry. *Cincinnatus*. Garden City, N.Y.: Doubleday, 1984.
Wood, Gordon S. *Revolutionary Characters*. New York: Penguin, 2006.

PHILLIS WHEATLEY

In every human breast, God has implanted a principle, which we call love of freedom

Gates, Henry Louis. *The Trials of Phillis Wheatley*. New York: Basic, 2003.
Robinson, William H. *Phillis Wheatley and Her Writings*. New York: Garland, 1984.
Robinson, William H. *Phillis Wheatley in the Black American Beginnings*. Detroit, Mich.: Broadside, 1975.
Shields, John C., ed. *The Collected Works of Phillis Wheatley*. New York: Oxford University Press, 1988.
Wheatley, Phillis. *Complete Writings*. Edited by Vincent Carretta. New York: Penguin, 2001.

Wheatley, Phillis. *The Poems of Phillis Wheatley.* Edited by Julian D. Mason. Chapel Hill: University of North Carolina Press, 1989.

JAMES WILSON

We the people

Ackerman, Bruce. *We the People.* Cambridge, Mass.: Belknap, 1991.

Amar, Akhil Reed. *America's Constitution.* New York: Random House, 2005.

Beard, Charles A. *An Economic Interpretation of the Constitution of the United States.* New York: Macmillan, 1960. Originally published in 1913.

Berkin, Carol. *A Brilliant Solution.* New York: Harcourt, 2002.

Bernstein, Richard B. with Kym S. Rice. *Are We to Be a Nation?* Cambridge, Mass.: Harvard University Press, 1987.

Farrand, Max. *The Framing of the Constitution of the United States.* New Haven, Conn.: Yale University Press, 1913.

Hall, Mark David. *The Political and Legal Philosophy of James Wilson.* Columbia: University of Missouri Press, 1997.

McDonald, Forrest. *We the People.* Chicago: University of Chicago Press, 1958.

McGuire, Robert A. *To Form a More Perfect Union.* New York: Oxford University Press, 2003.

Morgan, Edmund S. *Inventing the People.* New York: W. W. Norton, 1988.

Nedelsky, Jennifer. *Private Property and the Limits of American Constitutionalism.* Chicago: The University of Chicago Press, 1990.

Rakove, Jack N. *Original Meanings.* New York: Knopf, 1997.

Read, James H. *Power versus Liberty.* Charlottesville: University Press of Virginia, 2000.

Rossiter, Clinton. *1787.* New York: MacGibbon & Kee, 1966.

Smith, Charles Page. *James Wilson.* Chapel Hill: University of North Carolina Press, 1956.

Wood, Gordon S. *The Creation of the American Republic.* Chapel Hill: University of North Carolina Press, 1969.

*I*NDEX

235

𝒜BOUT THE 𝒜UTHOR

Paul Aron is senior editor at the Colonial Williamsburg Foundation. He is the author of *Unsolved Mysteries of American History*, *Unsolved Mysteries of History*, *Count the Ways*, *More Unsolved Mysteries of American History*, and *Did Babe Ruth Call His Shot?*

The Colonial Williamsburg Foundation is a private, not-for-profit organization that preserves and operates the 301-acre Historic Area as well as museums and educational outreach programs.